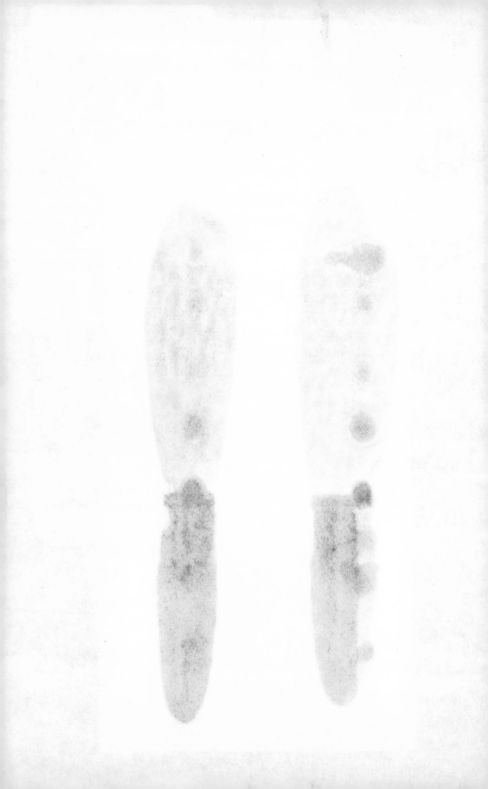

How to Get Your CREDITORS OFF YOUR BACK
without Losing Your Shirt

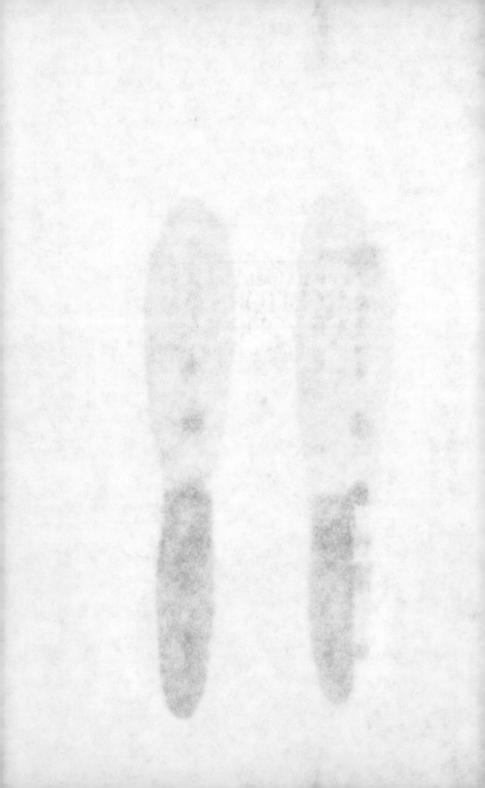

How to Get Your
CREDITORS
OFF YOUR BACK
without Losing Your Shirt

MELVIN J. KAPLAN
Attorney-at-Law
with PHILLIP T. DROTNING

Contemporary Books, Inc.
Chicago

Library of Congress Cataloging in Publication Data

Kaplan, Melvin James.
   How to get your creditors off your back without
losing your shirt.

    Includes index.
    1. Consumer credit—United States.   2. Consumer
credit—Law and legislation—United States.   3. Bank-
ruptcy—United States.   4. Finance, Personal.
I. Drotning, Phillip T., joint author. II. Title.
HG3756.U54K37   1979   346'.73'078   79-50971
ISBN 0-8092-7327-6
ISBN 0-8092-7326-8 pbk.

Published by Contemporary Books, Inc.
180 North Michigan Avenue, Chicago, Illinois 60601
Manufactured in the United States of America
Library of Congress Catalog Card Number: 79-50971
International Standard Book Number: 0-8092-7327-6 (cloth)
                           0-8092-7326-8 (paper)
Published simultaneously in Canada by
Beaverbooks
953 Dillingham Road
Pickering, Ontario L1W 1Z7
Canada

Contents

"If thou buy a Hebrew servant, six years shall he serve and in the seventh he shall go free."

—Exodus 21:2

"At the end of every seven years thou shalt make a release . . . every creditor that lendeth ought unto his neighbor shall release it, he shall not exact it of his neighbor, or of his brother, for it is the 'Lord's' release."

—Deuteronomy 15:2

Introduction

The combined impact of inflation, high taxes, and rising interest rates, compounded by imprudent use of easy credit, is driving millions of American families to financial disaster. The traumatic consequences of widespread insolvency are reflected in health statistics, divorce rates, case loads in family counseling services, and the dockets in bankruptcy court.

As an attorney specializing in personal financial counseling and bankruptcy law, I am visited each day by a stream of potential clients who open the conversation, often tearfully, with the plea, "Mr. Kaplan, I'm at my wit's end. . . ." Most of them are, indeed, at their wit's end, but almost without exception they have permitted the consequences of insolvency to become far more traumatic than they need to be.

Most of those who come to me for help are individuals and families who, for one reason or another, have accumulated obligations that, coupled with their basic living expenses, exceed their income. Rarely have they been spendthrifts. Even more rarely are they dishonest. And almost without exception they are horrified by their inability to make ends meet and would like to repay those who have granted them credit.

For the most part they come to me, not to escape their obligations, but to obtain relief from the consequences of their inability to pay everyone on time. Usually they have gone through months of harassment by bill collectors, their telephone ringing at all hours of the day and night. They have been verbally assaulted and abused. In some cases their neighbors and relatives have experienced the same treatment. Judgments have been obtained against them. Wage assignments have been executed. Their automobile is in hiding, to avoid repossession. And now—the last straw—they are behind on their mortgage payments and foreclosure is threatened.

In the back of their minds, throughout much of this ordeal, has been an awareness of bankruptcy as an escape from their dilemma. Until now, it has been rejected because of the social stigma and damage to their reputation they feared would result. "How could we ever face the neighbors," they ask themselves, overlooking the probability that their neighbors are already aware of their plight.

And so, at last, they come to me, prepared to accept bankruptcy as the last resort. They abhor the idea, but by now any solution that will enable them to escape the hassle that is driving them up the wall is acceptable.

And then comes the surprise! Most of the time they don't have to go through bankruptcy after all. Other options are open to them that end the harassment, enable them to resolve their financial problems—and do it without the humiliation experienced by visitors to bankruptcy court.

This is a book about bankruptcy, and more important, about those other choices; about the ways in which most people can get out of financial trouble without going bankrupt. It will tell you how you can stop your creditors—right now—from making any more threatening telephone calls. It will tell you how you can stop the interest payments and finance charges on the money you owe. It will tell you how to halt repossessions, garnishments, and foreclosures, void judgments that are outstanding against you, and get out of debt without materially reducing your standard of living. It will tell you how to do all this without losing your car, your furniture, your house, your savings and insurance, and without compromising your job.

Sound unreal? It isn't. All of these things are made possible by the Bankruptcy Reform Act of 1978, which became effective on October 1, 1979. Everything you need to know about it is right here in this book.

If you're head over heels in debt and see no way to escape the agony and embarrassment that befall those who can't pay their bills, you'll find the solution to your problem in the pages that follow.

Melvin James Kaplan
Chicago, Illinois
October 1, 1979

How to Get Your
CREDITORS
OFF YOUR BACK
without Losing Your Shirt

1

The perils of easy credit

In Grandpa's day the use of credit was limited, for the most part, to dire emergencies or the purchase of major necessities, such as a house. Anything not required for survival was regarded as a "luxury," to be enjoyed only when it could be paid for with surplus cash. Consumer debt was minimal and those who did owe money and failed to pay were viewed with contempt.

On our way to becoming a consumer society those values disappeared, along with many others that Grandpa held dear. The extent to which we have developed a credit economy is revealed in figures supplied by the Federal Reserve Board of Atlanta. During the last two years (1977 and 1978) American consumers have been borrowing at a rate of *more than $500 billion a year*. Furthermore, according to Patricia Falkenberry, a Federal Reserve economist,

American families have accumulated debts "far faster than
their financial resources have expanded."

Consumer credit in 1978 increased about 50 percent
from the level of 1975 and mortgage debt was up more
than 50 percent. In the first quarter of 1979 credit grew at a
15 percent annual rate. *Business Week* termed the increase
a "credit explosion so wild and so eccentric that it dwarfs
even the borrowing binge of the early 1970s."

Between 1963 and 1977 the share of after-tax personal
income that went to repay debts hovered around 20 percent. This is generally considered to be an acceptable level
for an individual or family. Unfortunately, however, even
at that level the cumulative figures did not reveal the
potentially explosive trouble that lurked within them.
They concealed the fact that many families were so deeply
in debt that their affairs had become unmanageable. Their
statistical presence was concealed by other families that
owed nothing at all.

Household debt at record high

Beginning in 1978, the situation got measurably worse.
In the third quarter the Townsend-Greenspan economic
consulting firm calculated that the ratio of household debt
payments to cash disposable income reached 25 percent—a
record high. Again, this figure distorted the real picture,
because about one-fifth of households had no debts at all.
Thus the overall portion of income required to service
debts, among those who had debts, was closer to one-third.
Inevitably, this means that many families in that group
are allocating half or more of their take-home pay to
servicing past debts. The ratio of total new borrowing to
take-home pay also rose to a peak of 3.1 percent in the
fourth quarter of 1978.

On the positive side, the growth of consumer credit in
the United States has been largely responsible for the

overall affluence of our citizens, the standard of living that we enjoy, and the level of economic growth that the nation has achieved. Destroy that credit system and our economy would suffer a severe—if not devastating—jolt. Our industrial machine, and the jobs and income it provides, are dependent on credit buying to absorb the goods that are produced. That's why indexes of "consumer confidence" are always cited by those attempting to predict the future course of the national economy. "Consumer confidence" really means the extent to which consumers are willing to go into debt to buy things they could do without.

On the negative side, there is considerable concern and an abundance of evidence to suggest that things are getting out of hand. Too many Americans are getting into debt over their heads. The condition of those who owe more than their share of the nation's personal debts is reflected in loan delinquencies, which are now running about double the 1963 rate. Mortgage payment delinquencies are also rising, even though the mortgage debt is one of the first to be paid by families that don't have enough money to cover all their bills. On the basis of the data that are available, the authors estimate that more than one in 25 homeowners are now at least a month behind in their mortgage payments.

According to the American Bankers Association, installment debt delinquencies rose to an unadjusted 2.71 percent of all accounts in December 1978, approaching the record 3.13 percent that was reached prior to the last recession. Bank credit card delinquencies, which represent nearly 10 percent of all installment credit, have also been rising at a rate that one industry observer calls "an explosive situation." H. Spencer Nilson, publisher of a credit card newsletter, the Nilson Report, told the *Wall Street Journal* in mid-1978: "Never before in our time have there been so many cards, so many lines of credit that exceed people's ability to pay."

The rising tide of financial difficulties shows up, too, in another statistic which probably also measures the level of harassment to which debtors are being subjected. In 1978 the number of accounts turned over to bill collectors rose 5 percent, from 42.2 million to 44.4 million. Although 44 million accounts does not mean 44 million debtors, because many are in trouble over more than one account, the figure still offers an appalling clue to the magnitude of consumer credit problems in America. The amount of money in the accounts turned over for collection rose even higher, up 10 percent from $4.36 billion to $4.78 billion.

Bankruptcies, only tip of iceberg

Finally, personal bankruptcies are now running at about 30 times the rate in 1947, increasing from 8,600 in that year to 250,000 in 1975. Filings fell off somewhat in 1978, but it is anticipated that the new phenomenon of lawyer advertising, the state of the economy, and the new benefits to the debtor incorporated in the new bankruptcy code will produce a dramatic escalation in bankruptcy filings in 1979 and the years ahead. The fact is that those presently finding their way to bankruptcy court are only the "tip of the iceberg." For every person who seeks relief through the courts there are hundreds of others who are experiencing the stresses and strains of overindebtedness and are searching for a solution.

Even a mild recession could also provoke a surge in bankruptcy filings. Many would be forced to file because of reduced income or the loss of jobs. Others would find themselves in trouble because of the indirect effects of the slowdown in the economy. Creditors who have been lenient while business was booming will begin to experience cash flow problems of their own, and become less tolerant of delinquencies and inability to pay. When the squeeze is on, many families that have been barely coasting along won't be able to do so anymore.

Many consumers are shocked by the change in personality that some merchants undergo when their customers fail to pay their bills. The genial character who coaxed or coerced them into buying the living room set in the first place suddenly becomes a vicious adversary who calls them deadbeats or worse, and excoriates them repeatedly for failure to pay.

The paradox in this situation is that those who have done most to encourage consumers to apply contemporary economic values to their borrowing habits are the first to invoke Grandpa's ground rules when their customers can't pay their bills. For the most part the burgeoning consumer debt and the inevitable delinquencies are the result of promotional efforts by the nation's business and financial institutions. Advertising that portrays the consumer as deprived if he doesn't vacation in Hawaii, gamble in Las Vegas, drive a Cadillac (you may be closer to owning one than you think!), and own appliances that will perform every chore that must be undertaken by man, has led to a psychology of entitlement. Everyone is *entitled* to have everything that anyone else has, and if you can't afford it, what the hell. "Buy now, pay later," has replaced "E Pluribus Unum" as the national watchword.

Americans pressured to borrow more

Reflect on your own experience and you'll realize the tremendous pressure that is applied to encourage Americans to spend more than they earn. Turn on the radio and friendly Bob Adams is waiting, money in hand, to finance the vacation you can't really afford. Open your VISA card statement and you'll find, along with the computer-induced warning that your payment is one month late, a sheaf of enticing folders that urge you to get even further behind.

Montgomery Ward & Company, on its billing statements, beseeches its customers to use their remaining credit, and even calculates the difference between their current balance and their credit line. The bank charge plans also cite "available credit," to encourage cardholders to use their charge privileges up to the hilt. The examples go on and on.

Small wonder that many families are tempted to get in over their heads!

To compound the problem, the blandishments to borrow more have been accompanied by development of some remarkably easy ways of doing it. Anyone over 40 can remember a time when credit purchases were limited primarily to the family home, one automobile, and the installment purchase of major appliances such as a washer and dryer or TV. Down payments were substantial and repayment periods fairly short. The family's remaining credit was probably confined to a few department stores where they had troubled to open an account.

Over the years, down payments dwindled and finally disappeared, and repayment periods lengthened to the point that 48-month auto loans have become common and 54 to 60 months not unusual. Household Finance Corp. says that the average maturity of its loans was 53 months in 1978, compared with 39 months in 1974. The longer payment periods, of course, are designed to appeal to those who are more concerned with the monthly payment than with the cost of the loan. Unfortunately, these are also the people who are usually skating on the flimsiest financial ice.

Alas, then came the bank charge card, those plastic magic carpets that will carry anyone to the land of his dreams. For too many charge card users the dreams became nightmares, for the bits of plastic were the curse of the impulse buyer who suddenly found himself equipped with charge privileges at almost any shop in every corner of the world. It soon became evident that many cardholders don't equate their card with money. Many push the thought of a day of reckoning to the back of their minds, and rack up huge charge card balances a few dollars at a time. To verify this phenomenon you need only observe the number of bank card charges of less than $5 that are made in the K-Mart checkout line.

Overdraft protection—a new temptation

During the early years of the bank charge menace there were some effective restraints on those tempted to buy today and worry about whether they could pay for it tomorrow. Every card imposed a credit limit, so once you had reached it on all of your cards your buying spree was over. Overdrafts and bounced checks were frowned on, so those who had no money in their purses or pockets and none in the bank were compelled to resist temptation, until payday, at least. Today, with the advent of automatic loans to cover checking account overdrafts, even that protection is gone. When Mrs. Consumer has reached her credit limit and there's no money left in the bank, who's to worry? She doesn't have to deny herself that new blouse, or even have to go to the bank to borrow the money. She simply writes a bum check and when it's presented, it's covered by the bank.

Some bankruptcy lawyers, viewing the pressures that Americans are under to spend more than they earn, maintain that the debtor who goes bankrupt is simply handing his creditors the fate that they deserve. A majority of attorneys, consulted by clients who are in financial trouble, will immediately recommend bankruptcy as the solution to their problems, without even discussing some of the less drastic alternatives that may be appropriate. One East Coast lawyer was quoted as saying:

"A person continually paying out more than 20 percent

of his income for past debts is fighting a losing battle and only prolongs the misery in an inevitable financial disaster."

That seems to be a more elaborate way of saying, "Only a sucker pays his debts."

But it doesn't even take a lawyer to push a consumer into bankruptcy. On the West Coast, do-it-yourself bankruptcy kits have proliferated. Inflammatory advertisements, designed to appeal to debtors who are angry, frustrated, and often irrational because of pressure from creditors, urge them to file their own bankruptcy petitions. Here's an example of one of those ads:

"All you need is $50 and file a petition showing all of your assets, liabilities, income, the names of creditors, and the amount owed to each. As soon as you file for bankruptcy you don't have to take any crap from anybody. If you had any garnishees on your salary, they come right off and you get a full paycheck. If a creditor dares to call you, make threats, tell the judge, who will give the culprit one warning and throw him in the slammer. All creditors are prohibited by law from contacting the debtor who has filed bankruptcy. That is a poetically sensitive law."

This description of bankruptcy is simplified to the point of being an almost blatant misrepresentation. We'll go into the hazards of filing your own bankruptcy in a later chapter, but for the moment let's just say that, while bankruptcy is appropriate and necessary in some cases, there are usually better ways to handle financial problems.

Nevertheless, the probabilities that bankruptcies will increase dramatically in the years ahead are very high. As the social stigma attached to bankruptcy lessens, more and more financially troubled consumers will decide that it is the best thing for them to do. They will be encouraged by the changes made in the Bankruptcy Reform Act, which substantially reduce the penalties that a bankrupt must endure.

God help us all if we reach the point where taking bankruptcy at the first sign of financial trouble becomes a respectable thing to do. It could destroy our credit system and produce the most colossal economic upheaval this country has ever endured.

If you're in financial trouble, consider other options less damaging to you and to the country before you choose bankruptcy as the only way out.

2
Who are the victims?

Many individuals and families have overextended themselves through imprudent use of easy credit. They simply couldn't resist temptation as long as the plastic pot of gold in their wallets still worked. But the vast majority of those in financial trouble are there through no fault of their own. True, they may have used their credit privileges to the outer limits of their ability to repay, but the debts were manageable at the time they were incurred.

Most young families are finding that it is a real struggle to establish themselves during an inflationary era when housing costs have doubled and tripled, and sirloin steak is so expensive that it has come to be regarded as an investment rather than an expense. Many are finding it necessary to commit an unreasonably large portion of their income to housing costs, and most find it difficult, if not impossible, to accumulate an emergency fund.

While Joe and Jan are both working, they are able to manage reasonably well, using their combined income to service the debt for their automobiles, household furnishings, and mortgage payments. They even manage to squeeze out the money to vacation in Florida for a week or two. But then their family physician, beaming with pleasure, informs Jan that a baby is on its way. What should be an occasion for rejoicing proves to be a disaster instead. Joe and Jan have developed a standard of living that depends on their combined income. With only Joe working they can't conceivably manage all of their debts.

The reality of their situation may escape them during the first flush of pleasure over the prospect of parenthood. Jan, they reason, can continue to work almost to the moment when the baby is due to arrive. They can give up a lot of the frills that their dual income made possible, and as a last resort Joe can always get a second, part-time job.

Alas, their confidence is short-lived. Jan has a near-miscarriage in the third month and has to quit her job. Most of the frills they planned to give up turn out to be installment purchases that can't be returned. Joe's salary isn't enough to cover their fixed obligations, and they've got the medical expenses to face on top of that. They begin to use their Mastercharge to purchase necessities that they once paid for with cash, but they soon fall behind on those payments, too, and their charge privileges are revoked.

Joe gets a consolidation loan

Desperate, Joe responds to a radio commercial touting one of the small loan companies that promise to solve their problems with a debt consolidation loan. He is surprised at how simple it is. He signs a wage assignment and a chattel mortgage on their furniture and within 24 hours his bills have been paid. Instead of a dozen creditors hounding him he now has—other than his car and the mortgage—only one creditor to pay: the finance company for the debt consolidation loan.

True, the payment isn't that much smaller than the combination of payments that it replaced, but it is manageable, and all of the past due bills are out of the way. He and Jan begin to breathe easily for the first time in months. With his part-time job they'll be able to make it, and in a few months Jan can go back to work and things will be rosy again.

But then the family auto conks out. Its ailment proves to be fatal and Joe must replace it in order to get to his part-time job. The payment throws the budget out of kilter again, but they'll manage somehow. And they just might have, except that the baby gets sick, and more medical expenses descend on them. To stay afloat, they begin using their credit cards again. Joe, worried about the baby, misses so much work that he loses his part-time job.

Soon they fall behind in their payments to the finance company that granted the consolidation loan. They are warned that the wage assignment may be exercised, or the chattel mortgage on their furniture foreclosed. They are also in arrears on their car payments, and repossession is a certainty if they don't come up with some money soon. Joe is beside himself, fearing that if the wage assignment is exercised he may lose his job.

Jan is also distraught because creditors have been phoning at all hours of the day and night. Once again, they're behind with everyone. She dreads the arrival of the mailman, knowing that the best news he can bring will be no news, instead of another threatening demand. When the doorbell rings she debates whether to answer it, fearing that another bill collector may be waiting outside. She's also worried about Joe, who has begun coming home after dark, parking his car two blocks from their house in the hope that the finance company won't be able to find it if they try to repossess. Both Joe and Jan are so emotionally drained that they aren't even able to enjoy the baby. They don't know it, but subconsciously they see him as the source of their troubles.

With some variations, this chain of events is one that has been and is being experienced by hundreds of thousands of Joes and Jans. But it is not only those who have experienced personal misfortunes who are in trouble. Many couples, despite a flourishing economy, have been caught in a financial crunch during the recent inflationary years. Consumers who borrowed yesterday can't pay today because they were tiptoeing a narrow ledge between solvency and financial disaster, and inflation has toppled them into an economic abyss.

Food prices have doubled

The official consumer price index reveals that the cost of the food that Americans eat at home has more than doubled in the last 10 years. Prices for meat, poultry, fish, coffee, and many other items have soared more than that. Five years ago a family of four could give mother respite from the kitchen, and enjoy a Big Mac, fries, and a milk shake for $4.20. Today the tab for the same items is over $8. The price of a chocolate bar has gone up 162 percent in 10 years. Such basic needs as potatoes and toilet paper have risen over 160 percent in the same period of time.

Nor is the end in sight. *U.S. News and World Report,* in 1978, reported that if prices in the ensuing five years increase at the rate of the previous five, these increases will occur by 1983:

- Shopping cart of food—up 54 percent, from $50 to $77.
- New car—up 38 percent, from $5,000 to $6,875.
- A day in the hospital—up 79 percent, from $100 to $179.
- A year in college—up 49 percent, from $5,200 to $7,740.
- Electric bill—up 58 percent, from $100 to $158.

The magazine also noted that to maintain their buying power after paying federal taxes, a married couple earning $15,000 a year in 1973 needed $22,452 in 1978, and will need $35,280 in 1983. The same family with a 1973 income of $25,000 needed $38,211 in 1978 and will need $61,744 five years after that. Americans will be fortunate if the actual experience by 1983 is not worse than that, for the calculation assumed an annual inflation rate of only 6.5 percent. The actual rate in 1979 was running much higher than that.

Meanwhile, the energy crunch is compounding the problem, and nobody knows what the future holds. The increased costs of gasoline, home heating, and utility bills have already been enough to drive many families to the wall. This Arabian nightmare is particularly menacing because it involves necessities that no family can do without. As the costs of necessities advance, families with marginal incomes are compelled to borrow to stay afloat, adding exorbitant interest costs to their basic expenses. Inevitably, they find themselves falling further and further behind.

No "typical" bankrupt

I am often asked to describe the "typical" bankrupt. Is there an average amount that the bankrupt owes at the time he files, or an average income range among those who file? The answer to both questions is "No." I have seen bankruptcies filed by secretaries with incomes of $8,000 a year, and have filed many for individuals making fifty, sixty, and even seventy thousand dollars a year. You don't have to be poor to live beyond your means, and the affluent two-income family which has established a standard of living at that level is particularly vulnerable if one of the members is suddenly without a paycheck.

It would be misleading to suggest that financial difficulties stem only from personal misfortunes such as divorce, pregnancy, illness, unemployment, or being a good samaritan and guaranteeing loans for relatives and friends. There are classic cases—types of people who are constantly in trouble because of psychological hangups of their own. They include:

Impulse buyers, who are compelled to buy things to satisfy some psychological need, even though they don't have the money to pay for them and often don't even want or need the things that they buy. Many of them are only one step removed from kleptomania, because they take the merchandise knowing that they won't be able to pay.

Dreamers, who have no concept of money management principles, and get themselves into grave financial difficulty without realizing that they are doing so, or the consequences of what they have done. They don't seem to realize that if they can't afford to buy a $1,000 item, they certainly can't afford to pay $1,500 for it a little at a time.

Chronic gamblers and alcoholics, who will resort to any action or deceit to obtain the money that their compulsion demands.

Of the group, the gamblers and alcoholics probably get the least sympathy and deserve the most. Not only are they the victims of expensive habits, but the habits cause them to experience many of the personal misfortunes caused by pregnancy, illness, or unemployment.

I dwell on debtors in these classic situations because, in all candor, the solutions recommended in this book may not be helpful to them. None of the current approaches to resolving financial problems, whether they be court solutions or other methods, are absolute in cases that are rooted in psychological problems. The traditional approach to debt problems—debt management, budget counseling, Chapter 13, or bankruptcy—will not work for the chronic gambler, the alcoholic, the dreamer, the impulse buyer, or the compulsive spender. If your case fits in one of these categories, be advised that psychological therapy is needed in conjunction with the approaches described in this book.

The approach most lawyers take is to treat the symptoms without worrying about the causes. After all, they are not psychiatrists, and dealing with the symptoms is all they really have been asked to do. Filing bankruptcy or Chapter 13 for the compulsive spender may resolve the superficial external problem by easing the creditor pressure for the moment, but you can bet that it won't be long before the debtor is back in the same trouble he was in before.

Psychological help needed

The ultimate solution for these classic cases will probably require both legal and psychological help. We are trying to experiment with this in my practice, using group therapy to reach compulsive gamblers, alcoholics, dreamers, impulse buyers, and compulsive spenders. Our success has been limited by the reluctance of most financially troubled debtors to accept that they have one of these characteristics.

Let me emphasize again that, although these classic cases are not uncommon, the vast majority of individuals and families who come to me for help are not in any of these categories. Most of them have experienced some change in their personal circumstances that drove them to financial ruin. Most of them, too, have struggled manfully, if unskillfully and unwisely, to resolve their problems by themselves before seeking legal help. They have endured years of robbing Peter to pay Paul, juggling each paycheck to grease the wheels that are squeaking loudest. Often they have endured the most vicious forms of harassment by creditors and collection agencies, and have reached the point where their jobs or their homes are threatened before finally deciding to take any action that is necessary to get their creditors off their backs.

A bankruptcy judge, Emil Goldhaber of Philadelphia, says, "I'm amazed at how many people wind up in bankruptcy court with no assets and ten to fifteen thousand dollars in debt to lending institutions. I sometimes feel that people who come before my court have had credit jammed down their throats—and I don't blame them for going bankrupt."

There may be some consolation in that, but however much your creditors deserve it, the fact remains that bankruptcy also exacts its price from you. Your creditors may have lured you into the situation you are in, but you must assume responsibility, too, for the imprudence that led you to respond to their appeals. In my experience, most debtors in trouble believe their situation to be more hopeless than it is. For most of them, a solution short of bankruptcy can be found.

3

Facing reality

Most of us have known people with serious illnesses who have delayed seeing their doctors out of fear that their worst suspicions will be confirmed. So it is, too, with many individuals and families who are ailing financially; they sense that something is wrong, but avoid making a detailed diagnosis of their financial problems because of fear of what they will learn.

There are some early warning signs of financial trouble that should prompt an immediate, detailed review of your financial position. During the early stages of a developing financial crisis there may still be time to make adjustments that will help you avoid the disaster that is otherwise inevitable. Putting on blinders and hoping that the troubles will go away, or resorting to unplanned emergency measures to forestall creditors are the worst possible responses to the warning signs.

Warning signs

Here are some of the things that should alert you to financial troubles ahead:

- Difficulty in meeting rent or mortgage payments on time.
- Use of credit cards and charge accounts to supplement cash and extend income.
- Commitment of more than 25 percent of net monthly income for installment obligations.
- Inability to build reserve savings to meet unexpected emergencies.

Many families, confronted with these storm clouds on the financial horizon, react like a six-year-old to a thunderstorm. They pull the sheets over their heads and hope that when they awake the sun will be out and the world will be smiling at them again. The sheets they should resort to are the balance sheets that will tell them where they stand and what their options may be.

The alternative is a never-ending series of calamities, each a little more harrowing than the last.

Let's return to Joe and Jan and see where they went wrong. First, their response to their problems was governed by hope rather than reason. At no time did they construct a personal financial inventory that would reveal what their real situation was. Instead, they resorted to temporary measures to appease creditors and keep afloat until better days came along. Initially, they paid their most demanding creditors, and let their other bills slide. To gain added cash to meet current obligations they got cash advances on their bank cards, adding another monthly bill plus large interest charges to the shortfall they already had. When that source of funds was exhausted they turned to the small loan company, consolidating their debts, but adding one more interest payment to what they owed. When unexpected expenses made it impossible for them to pay the small loan company they began using their other accounts again, and soon were in deeper trouble than they had ever been before.

Couple adept at deception

Like other desperate debtors, they became adept at deception in their efforts to forestall creditors until the day when Jan could return to work and, they believed, their affairs would become manageable again. At first, when a creditor called, Jan resorted to the relatively innocent but time-worn assurance that "the check is in the mail." It wasn't, of course, but hopefully it would be before the creditor called again.

That worked at first, but not for long. Any creditor will tell you that this phrase is so common it may have surpassed "close cover before striking" as the most-used phrase in the English language. When it didn't work any more, Jan and Joe tried a new tactic. Instead of paying their most persistent creditors in full, they sent small partial payments to everyone on the list. Because most creditors regard this as evidence of some intention to pay, it worked for a while, but meanwhile all of the couple's accounts fell further and further behind. Ultimately, the creditors began to demand payment in full.

When they were threatened with lawsuits, Joe and Jan

promised to pay, knowing as they made the promises that they couldn't keep them. They bought time with a variety of ruses. They mailed unsigned checks, gaining a few days while the checks were returned for signature. They wrote checks on which the numerical and written amounts did not agree, making the difference large enough so the bank would return them for correction. This gained a few more days.

Taking a lesson from the corporation that employed him, Joe then opened checking accounts in several distant cities. He paid his bills with checks drawn on banks that were farthest from the creditor's offices. This bought time while the checks traveled across the country, going through the clearing process.

Joe, fortunately, didn't ever reach the stage of employing devices that were downright illegal, although in desperation some debtors do. They pay bills with checks drawn on Bank A, and then close the account and transfer their funds to Bank B. When creditors complain about the bouncing checks, the debtor says, innocently, "We had some trouble at the bank and decided to make a change. I'm sorry your check got caught in the mail." Or, they insist that the bill was paid, and when proof is demanded they alter the date on a check for a previous payment, make a photocopy, and offer it as proof that the payment was made.

Beating the computer

Joe and Jan did neither of these things, although, had they been aware of another, made possible by the computer age, they might have tried it. The debtor employs a little gadget to demagnetize the ink in the Federal Reserve transit number and account number that appear on the

face of his checks. This causes the bank's computer to
reject the check which then, by law, must be sorted by
hand. Since most banks have reduced the staffs available
for hand work, the check may take up to three weeks to
clear.

The bottom line of the subterfuges that Joe and Jan did
employ was still an ultimate need to face reality. They
should have done it at the outset, when it still might have
been possible to secure their creditors' approval of an
orderly, voluntary debt reduction plan. Now, instead, their
creditors were angrier than before. Jan and Joe were legiti-
mate prey for every legal means to exact payment from a
debtor whose actions have revealed that he doesn't intend
to pay. The resources available to them for this purpose
were, as Joe and Jan discovered, frightening to behold and
painful to endure.

Soon after its initial threat to exercise the wage assignment or foreclose the chattel mortgage on their furniture,
the loan company that had consolidated their debts sent
them a "Final Notice Before Intention of Demand Upon
Wage Assignment." (Fig. 1) This was simply a formal
warning that the creditor was about to exercise the wage
assignment they had agreed to in order to obtain the loan.

Joe and Jan were now on notice that if they failed to
remit the sum claimed within a specified period, further
action would be taken. They were unable to pay, and soon
received a "Notice of Intention to Make Demand on Employer." (Fig. 2) This time Joe's employer also received a
copy of the notice, which advised that unless Joe and Jan
paid the amount owed within 20 days, or entered a defense
against the wage assignment, a demand would be made on
Joe's employer for assignment of his wages to pay the bill.
Joe was still unable to pay, and 20 days later the demand
was made (Fig. 3), and Joe was asked to pay a visit to his
supervisor.

COLLECTION DEPARTMENT
THIS IS FINAL NOTICE BEFORE INTENTION OF DEMAND ON ASSIGNMENT OF WAGES

Final Notice Before Intention of Demand Upon Wage Assignment

Chicago, Ill. ___Oct. 1___ ___1979___

Arrears $ ___168.00___

Balance $ ___800.00___

Acct. No. ___31349___

To ___Joe Roe___

___611 Center Street___

___Chicago Ill.___

Circumstances compel us to contemplate notifying your employer, after intention to make demand, of the assignment of your wages for the following account: ___Lane Jewelers___

Unless we receive, immediately the amount of arrears as shown above, this action will be instituted.

Very truly yours,

This is final and unconditional.

Acknowledged before me this ___1st___

day of ___October___ ___, 1979___

_____
NOTARY PUBLIC

LOU HARRIS & CO.
343 S. DEARBORN STREET
SUITE 1102 CHICAGO, ILL. 60604
WAbash 2-1759

By ___Lou Harris___
COLLECTION DEPARTMENT

DO NOT NEGLECT THIS NOTICE

Figure 1 Sample of dunning notice received by debtors

NOTICE OF INTENTION TO MAKE DEMAND ON EMPLOYER

To: Joe Roe
611 Center Street
Chicago, Ill.

You are hereby notified that the undersigned creditor intends to make a demand upon your employer upon a wage assignment executed by you on the   1st   day of   May   , 19 79 , to secure a debt contracted on the   15th   day of   May   1979   in the amount of $1000.00   on which there has been paid $ 200.00

The terms of the contract are   24   payments at $42.00

You are now in default on such indebtedness in the amount of $ 168.00   , the last payment having been made on the   15th   day of   June   , 1979 .

Within 20 days after the receipt of this notice you may notify your employer, and the undersigned creditor, in writing under oath, of any defenses you may have to said wage assignment. In the event a false defense is made you will be subject to the payment of attorney's fees, costs and other damages, if any.

Dated this   1st   day of   Oct.   1979

....

LANE JEWELERS
16 W. VAN BUREN
CHICAGO, ILLINOIS 60605
HA 7-1280

Figure 2   Sample of notice of intent to make wage demand

LANE JEWELERS

16 W. VAN BUREN ST. — CHICAGO, ILL. 60605

Phone HArrison 7-1280

Statutory Notice of Assignment of Wages

RE: Joe Roe

TO: D.D.T. Trucking Company

333 E River Street

Chicago Ill.

OUR ACCOUNT NO 31349

CLOCK NO 36

OCCUPATION - Driver

Demand is hereby made upon you upon an assignment of salary, wages, commisions or other compensation for services executed by Joe Roe and delivered to LANE JEWELERS on the 1st day of May ,1979 , to secure a debt contracted on the 1st day of May , 1979. The total amount of the debt ls $1000 00. Payment in the amount of $200.00 have been made. The duration of the contract is 24 months. There is now due and owing without acceleration the sum of $ 800.00 , the last payment having been made on the 1st day of June , 1979.

The employee herein named has been in default in his payments in the amount of $ 42.00 of which $168 has been due and owing for more than 40 days. Unless you have received within the past 20 days, or do receive within 2 days after the service hereof, a notice of defense from the employee herein named, you are required by law to make payment in accordance with such assignment.

By Lou Harris

LANE JEWELERS
16 W. VAN BUREN STREET
CHICAGO, ILLINOIS 60605
HA 7-1280

STATE OF ILLINOIS
COUNTY OF Cook.

Barry Smith first being duly sworn, deposes and says that the facts stated in the Demand above are true and correct; and further deposes and says that he has no notice of any defenses of the debtor.

Subscribed and sworn to before me this 20th day of Oct 1979

....
Notary Public

*Sec. 3 of the Wage Assignment Act provides: "No assignment of wages shall become invalid by cessation of employment, but shall be valid and collectible against any future employer of the wage-earner within a period of 2 years from the date of its execution."

"The labor of services are those of the individual. The wages of salary to be earned are HIS property. The right to dispose of them at such time, for such consideration, and upon such terms as he sees fit, are his."

Figure 3 Sample of demand for assignment of wages

Wage assignment a turning point

That request proved to be the turning point for Joe and Jan. Joe's boss expressed disappointment that Joe was unable to manage his financial affairs, and suggested that the company viewed wage assignments and garnishments with great displeasure. While the law prevented them from firing him for this reason, the incident would certainly effect his career if he were unable to resolve his problems quickly. Then, somewhat more sympathetically, the supervisor told Joe that he regarded him as a valuable employee. Perhaps it would help, he suggested, if Joe and Jan were to visit a counselor for assistance in straightening out their affairs and resolving their debts.

Joe, curiously elated, rushed home to Jan. The worst had happened and he still had his job! Even more important, his boss had suggested an avenue that offered a ray of hope. He had given him the name of an attorney who specialized in family financial counseling, and Joe could hardly wait for morning to make the call.

Joe could count himself among the lucky ones, for he got started on the right track before everything got completely out of hand. No one had yet filed a judgment against him. Although he was behind on his mortgage payments, no foreclosure proceedings had been filed. Although repossession had been threatened, he still had his car. Most important, none of his other creditors had yet resorted to garnishment in their efforts to make him pay. Joe knew that, although the law prevents an employer from dismissing an employee because of a garnishment, other reasons can usually be found to discharge a debt-plagued employee if the employer chooses to do so.

Joe would avoid that disaster because someone had pointed out the way in time.

4

How to construct a personal financial inventory

The cash flow problems experienced by most individuals and families begin to reveal themselves at a point when further trouble could be avoided by simple and relatively painless adjustments in living style. The necessary adjustments are possible, however, only if you know precisely where you stand. Where financial problems are concerned, wishful thinking is no substitute for thoughtful planning.

At the first sign of financial trouble, a thorough and detailed financial inventory should be made. There is nothing really complicated about it. Simply draw up a balance sheet that reflects, on one side, your income from all sources as it will be received throughout the year. For most families, this may be the regular paycheck and nothing more. Others may have dividend, rental, or other income that can be added to the pot.

On the other side of the ledger, record your average monthly expenditures for all purposes, and your fixed monthly obligations for rent or mortgage payments, automobile loans, and other installment payments. Don't forget anything and don't fudge—or your efforts will be an exercise in futility. Be thorough, and refrain from deceiving yourself. Include only that income which you are certain you will receive. Estimate your living expenses realistically. Include estimates of unusual expenses—doctor's and dentist's bills, for example—based on your experience the previous year. Estimate your transportation expenses with an eye on rising costs, and be sure to include probable maintenance expenses for your car. List all of your fixed monthly installment obligations, as well as other payments—such as insurance—that must be made periodically throughout the year.

When you have finished itemizing the income and expense sides of your ledger on a monthly basis, look at those quarterly, semiannual, or annual payments that you must make and add an amount to your monthly expenses sufficient to accrue what you will need to pay them when they fall due. Now total your monthly expenses and monthly income and see where you stand.

Presumably, since you already knew you were in trouble, your personal financial inventory will reveal that your expenses exceed what you earn. If so, the time to act is now.

Where can you cut down?

First, review your discretionary expenses and determine where you may be able to cut down. Can you shave your food budget by using fewer high-priced convenience items, and buying basic foods instead? Convenience foods save your time, of course, but that means someone else is doing your work for you, and you are paying for the time it takes them to do it. How much can you save by trying to restrict your purchases to items that are on sale, buying in-season fruits and vegetables, and making judicious use of discount coupons? What lower-priced meats can you substitute for steaks, roasts, and chops, in order to prepare less expensive meals?

Remember, when you visit the supermarket, that the aisles are deliberately arranged to appeal to the weaknesses of impulse buyers. *Never shop without a list,* and when you get to the store stick to it; don't be tempted to buy things you don't need. Finally, avoid the fancy grades and labels. The generic foods and house brands available in most stores are fully as nutritious as the more expensive advertised brands.

When you have reviewed your grocery expenditures, do the same thing with other discretionary expenditures such as clothing and entertainment. Then check your transportation costs. One of the paradoxes of the current inflationary era is the fact that when the price of coffee or steak goes out of sight, most families will use less, or turn to less costly substitutes. Not so, apparently, with gasoline. The American love affair with the automobile is such that despite steadily rising fuel costs, gasoline consumption is going up, too.

Surveys show that most families admit that 20 percent or more of their automobile trips are not essential to their needs. Most families can save substantially on gasoline, without major inconvenience, simply by foregoing unnecessary trips. The odds are that you can help save energy and save money, too, by planning your trips more carefully. Think ahead, combine your visits to the dentist, school, and the grocery store, and be surprised at the money that you save!

Your review of your living expenses will almost certainly convince you that you can live on considerably less than you thought. It may not be enough to balance your budget, but it certainly will help. Now it's time to review your monthly fixed obligations. Begin with housing, which should not be costing more than a quarter of your take-home pay. If you are spending substantially more than that, it may be the source of your troubles, and you should consider making a change that will bring this cost into line. What about automobiles? Are you driving a gas hog, or even two? Maybe it's time to forego luxury in favor of economy, and opt for the fuel savings of a less expensive high-mileage car.

Can you cut monthly payments?

What about your other monthly payments? Do you have installment or revolving charge accounts with finance charges in the 18 percent range? If so, consider whether there is a way they can be refinanced at a lower rate. Do you have a savings account you haven't wanted to touch? Perhaps you can consolidate all of your bills by using it as security for a lower cost loan. What about your life insurance policies? Is there a cash or loan value available that you can use? Life insurance loans are available at rates as low as 6 percent. It makes more sense to pay that to the insurance company than 18 percent to somebody else. Insurance loans also afford more flexibility in repayment because you do not have to commit yourself to monthly installments, or to any specific repayment date. The loan will remain in force until it is convenient for you to repay it.

Finally, don't overlook the credit union if you have one where you work. The interest rates are usually more favorable than those of banks and other lending institutions, and credit unions are often more lenient in granting credit because they have the advantage of payroll witholding to collect the required payments as they fall due. They are also managed by your coworkers, who are likely to be more sympathetic than a stranger at the bank.

Hopefully, if you aren't already in too critical a situation, this combination of adjustments will put you in a position to resolve your financial problems because your obligations no longer exceed your means. If not, it's time to look at the other options you may be able to employ.

5

Options for escaping the pressure cooker

Joe and Jan finally confronted their financial dilemma by visiting the attorney whom Joe's boss had recommended. It was really the only alternative in their case because they had already foreclosed, by their own behavior, the other options that could have been available to them. For others, once they have faced up to their problems and determined precisely where they stand, simpler methods may suffice.

If a calculated effort to curtail living expenses and reduce monthly payments, interest and finance charges by restructuring your debt are not sufficient to resolve your problems, you may be able to negotiate a manageable repayment schedule. This is probably feasible, however, only if you have not let things go so far, and established such a record of broken promises, that your credibility with your creditors has already been destroyed.

If you are not in that position, and your relationships with your creditors have not yet been severely damaged, they may be willing to accept a revised payment schedule that can be managed within the income that is at your disposal. They will be most receptive if your financial problems are temporary in nature, and there is a reasonable expectation that your situation will change for the better within a reasonable period of time—say a year. Remember, though, that such an arrangement will rise or fall on the basis that *all* of your creditors are willing to cooperate. If one or more of them refuses to go along, thus reducing the amount available to the others, there is little prospect that your efforts will meet with success.

How to negotiate with creditors

The best approach in negotiating a temporary moratorium on payments or a reduced payment plan is to visit each of your creditors and level with them about where you stand, and why you are experiencing financial difficulties. Show them your personal balance sheet, which reflects your present monthly commitments and the amount that is available to apply to them. Prepare, for their perusal, a proposal that provides an equitable share of the available sum to each of your creditors until your situation improves and you can resume full payments again. Make it clear to them, as sincerely as you can, that you want to pay your debts and intend to do so, but that you are clearly unable to pay everyone at the previously agreed rate from the money that is available. Tell them that you wish to avoid more drastic steps that have been suggested to you, such as bankruptcy, but that you obviously will have to consider them if you can't work out a viable repayment plan.

Most creditors, if they feel that there is a reasonable chance for voluntary repayment on your part, even at a reduced rate, would rather not invoke the means of collection that are available. The furniture store doesn't want to reclaim your furniture, because there is little possibility that they will be able to dispose of it for a sum that would cover the amount you owe. Besides, they regard repossession as an expensive nuisance and they are more likely to threaten it than to carry it out.

The same is true of your car and your home. With the minimum down payments and extended payment plans that prevail today, the depreciated value of an automobile is probably less than the amount you owe on it the moment you drive it off the lot. The nuisance and the cost of repossessing it make this action undesirable if there is any real prospect that you will ultimately pay your note in full.

For the bank or savings and loan that holds the mortgage on your home, foreclosure is an even less desirable option. The law, in most states, extends broad protections to the homeowner that allow him to remain in the foreclosed home for an extended period, and to retrieve it by catching up on his payments even after a foreclosure action has been filed. The costs to the lending institution for court fees and legal services are also formidable, to say nothing of the real estate commissions when they eventually are able to dispose of the home. Here, again, a workout plan that has a reasonable prospect of success is a more desirable alternative for them.

Beware of proraters

Many debtors, reluctant to approach their creditors to negotiate their own reduced payment plans, respond to ads inserted by "proraters" or seek help from nonprofit family financial counseling groups. They may be helpful in some cases, but a great deal of caution should be exercised before entering into an arrangement of this sort.

Under a typical prorating arrangement, the debtor enters into an agreement to pay the prorater a specific sum each payday. The prorater agrees to contact all creditors and make arrangements to distribute the sum among them until all of the debts have been retired. For this he receives a 10 to 15 percent fee. The system can work if all of the creditors are willing to agree to it, and if the debtor is consistent in making his payments to the prorater.

Unfortunately, over the years, many debtors have encountered unscrupulous proraters who have accepted the payments from the debtor, but failed to negotiate acceptance by all of the creditors. Ultimately, when the debtor is threatened by creditor lawsuits, he discovers that the prorater has accepted his money and collected his fee, but failed to live up to his part of the bargain.

Although proraters are regulated by state law in the few states where this kind of service is still legal, they too often are interested only in getting the debtor to sign a contract and make the payments from which they garner their fee. Repeatedly, I have seen cases where a debt prorater committed a debtor to make payments to creditors when, in fact, he wasn't earning enough to pay his fixed living expenses.

Non-profit consumer credit counseling services are more likely to offer real help to the debtor. First, there is little danger that they will operate outside the law and, second, they have a genuine interest in helping the debtor get back on his feet and meet his obligations. The problem with many of these services is an attitude and policy among most of them that *they will keep the debtor away from bankruptcy court no matter what*. Bankruptcy, in my judgment, should be avoided if better alternatives exist, but in some situations it is the only logical recourse for the debtor because the alternative is financial slavery.

This orientation on the part of the credit counseling services stems from the fact that many of them have been organized by the leading credit-granting institutions in the city, and most of them receive the bulk of their financial support from such organizations. Accordingly, the debtor who should be filing a bankruptcy petition or Chapter 13 repayment plan is lulled into a false sense of security. He is encouraged to commit all of his available disposable income to the consumer credit counselor each payday even though there is no way in which he can pay his bills and the continuing interest or service charges within any reasonable period of time. Ultimately, he will be driven to bankruptcy, but only after his creditors have extracted the last possible dime from his income, and he has submitted to a lengthy period of deprivation in the belief that, ultimately, everything will work out.

Conflict of interest?

There is a strong suggestion of conflict of interest when an agency represents itself as serving the needs of debtors but, in fact, must give attention to the interests of the creditors who are providing it with its financial support. In my experience, consumer credit counseling offices will seldom attempt to resolve a disputed obligation, or attempt to reduce or eliminate service charges or precomputed interest. Their purpose is to see that you cut your living costs to the bone to make every possible dollar available, ad infinitum, to the credit-granting companies from whom they derive their support.

A better approach, if all of the voluntary efforts of the debtor have failed to produce a solution, is to engage an attorney who specializes in this field. He can evaluate your financial position and if it is feasible act, in effect, as a debt prorater in your behalf. The advantage in this course of action is the fact that the attorney usually has more leverage than a prorating company or a consumer credit counseling office, particularly if the attorney is known to specialize in bankruptcies and Chapter 13. The creditors realize that if they accept a voluntary repayment plan, they may ultimately receive all that is due them. If they reject it, the debtor may file bankruptcy and they will get nothing, or they will be forced to settle for less than is due and wait longer for it because the debtor files under Chapter 13.

Your problem, if you choose this option, will be to find a lawyer who is willing to handle your case. Debt consolidation, even if an attorney were to impose a fee of 20 percent of all debts handled, would not produce a very lucrative practice. However, if there is a sufficient surplus in the family's income, after paying fixed living expenses, to retire all debts within eighteen months to two years, there is an alternative. This is a self-administered debt management program in which the attorney sets up a payment schedule with the creditors and the debtor fulfills this commitment on his own.

A program of this sort eliminates the costs the attorney would incur if he handled the money and were compelled to issue the checks and do the paperwork associated with the plan. It will work unless the debtor is unwilling or unable to exercise the discipline necessary to live on the budget that he has agreed to, and consequently is unable to adhere to the payment schedule. In that event, there may be no alternative but bankruptcy or Chapter 13.

Avoid bankruptcy if possible

In my judgment, the greatest service an attorney can perform for a debtor is to keep him out of bankruptcy court. Although the stigma associated with bankruptcy has diminished, it has not disappeared and some of the consequences of choosing this route may haunt the debtor for years. There are those who have filed bankruptcy and joke about it, but in their more serious moments will confess that the experience was just a few anguish points away from having root canal work done with a half-inch bit. A noted Chicago lawyer once told me, only half in jest, that bankruptcy has come to enjoy the same status as venereal disease, "socially acceptable but nothing to brag about."

A later chapter will deal with bankruptcy as a last resort, and you have certainly surmised by now that it is only in that context that it should be considered. Any other solution that is feasible in your case is certain to be less traumatic and less damaging to your own sense of self worth. That assertion assumes, of course, that like most Americans you are inherently honest and are searching for a way to pay your creditors, not a way to escape your debts.

If all out-of-court remedies fail, you or your attorney should consider recourse to Chapter 13. This is the section of the bankruptcy act, formerly known as the wage earner plan, under which you undertake payment of your creditors under the supervision of a court-appointed trustee, over a period that generally does not exceed three years. Under the new bankruptcy code it is available to any individual with a regular income.

The procedure under Chapter 13 requires that you file a repayment plan which may pay all of your creditors in full or may, under a composition plan, provide for payment of only a portion of the unsecured claims. Generally, the amounts owed are reduced by the amount of precomputed interest or finance charges that they include. Further, under the new bankruptcy act, the amount that must be repaid on secured claims will be based on the current market value of the security, and not on the amount owed. Thus, if you owe a furniture store a balance of three thousand dollars, including finance charges, the amount you actually would be required to pay would be the actual current value of the furniture with which the loan was secured. Chapter 13, in short, offers a means of eliminating your debts by paying your creditors under a court-approved plan and, while it is less desirable than resolving your problems by nonlegal means, it offers numerous advantages not enjoyed by those who opt for bankruptcy court.

How much does it cost?

First, there is the matter of expense. Attorney's fees for both consumer bankruptcy and Chapter 13 vary throughout the country. Minimum attorney's fees are no longer recommended by the local bar associations, so competition among debtor relief lawyers sets the going fee. Attorney's fees for consumer bankruptcy range anywhere from $150 to $2,500, depending upon the complexity of the case and the experience and qualifications of the bankruptcy attorney who is retained. Chapter 13 fees are more closely scrutinized than bankruptcy fees, and at the first meeting of creditors the attorney usually must reveal by affidavit the fee being charged, the amount already received, and any balance due which generally will be paid by the Chapter 13 trustee. Fees range from $150 up to $600, or slightly higher if it is a joint filing by husband and wife. In addition, the debtor will pay the standing trustee fees which may range up to 11 percent of all the funds disbursed.

To a debtor who already owes more than he can handle, these fees may seem only to compound his problem. They must be viewed in perspective if they are to make any sense. First of all, the total cost arising from lawyer's and trustee's fees in a Chapter 13 case is lower than what the debtor would have paid for a prime rate consolidation loan at a local bank. More significant, however, is the reduction in the total amount owed that probably will be achieved by filing Chapter 13. In the thousands of such cases that I have filed, I have yet to see one completed in which the debtor has not paid less than originally scheduled, even after paying all creditors who filed claims, plus the attorney's and trustee's fees. This is true because any creditor, to be eligible for repayment under the plan, must file his claim within six months after the first meeting of creditors, Typically, many creditors fail to file the claims, whereupon the debtor is discharged from paying the obligation.

The competent Chapter 13 attorney also is usually able to obtain substantial concessions in the existing balances owed to creditors by having all precomputed interest and service charges eliminated from the claim. Thus, payments by the Chapter 13 trustee will not be applied against service charges or interest, but only to the principal of the obligation that remains.

Creditors have no voice

Another substantial benefit to the Chapter 13 debtor is provided under the new bankruptcy code. It contains "cram-down" provisions that apply to secured creditors under which the debtor pays only the actual current value of the secured claim, as determined by the court, rather than the contract balance. This can save the debtor hundreds or even thousands of dollars because the actual value of the security may be only a fraction of the amount still owed.

Generally, to be acceptable to the court, a Chapter 13 plan must be one that can be completed within three years, although plans of four or five years duration are sometimes allowed. Presumably, the rationale is that a plan of longer duration amounts to indentured servitude, and if the disposable income of the debtor is not sufficient to complete the plan within three years, he should file bankruptcy instead.

In many cases, the obligations of the debtor may be so large, and the available resources for repayment so limited, that a plan cannot be devised that can be completed in three years. In such cases a "composition plan" may be proposed, in which the debtor does not assume responsibility for paying his creditors in full, but proposes to pay some percentage of the unsecured obligations instead. In some cases the amount proposed for unsecured creditors may be as little as 10 percent. Although such a plan may seem little short of actually declaring bankruptcy, it may receive court approval if it is shown that the amount received by the creditors will exceed what they would have realized from the assets if bankruptcy were declared.

Of particular concern to the client, when he and his attorney are considering the alternatives, are the personal consequences to the debtor if he opts for bankruptcy rather than Chapter 13. Although there is some question why anyone who finds himself in trouble because of credit should want more of it, the effect of bankruptcy and Chapter 13 on the debtor's credit rating is almost always a matter of concern.

Under the federal Truth in Lending Act, a bankruptcy may be kept on a debtor's credit record for a period of 14 years. Chapter 13 may remain on the credit bureau records for only seven years. However, some credit bureaus have adopted a policy of removing all adverse information from the debtor's file once they have received notice of the successful completion of a Chapter 13 plan. Only a note that a Chapter 13 has been successfully completed will remain. Some follow the same procedure when a bankruptcy is filed and a discharge entered. Some credit bureaus, however, list the fact that a Chapter 13 has been successfully completed, or a bankruptcy discharge entered, but continue to list all of the obligations of the debtor prior to the filings, whether they have been paid or not.

Attitudes toward bankruptcy

Many lending institutions, retail stores, banks, and loan companies refuse to do business with persons who have gone bankrupt, and many apply the same policy to those who have filed under Chapter 13. However, increasingly, institutions of this sort have begun to realize that there is a difference between debtors who choose bankruptcy and those who file under Chapter 13. The current trend is an increased willingness to extend credit to debtors who are successful in exercising the discipline to pay their bills over an extended period of time through Chapter 13. The Chapter 13 debtor has given evidence of his desire to pay his bills and, even more important, has demonstrated an ability to exercise self-discipline and manage his affairs that suggests he will probably handle future credit in a wiser and more responsible manner.

These more enlightened credit-grantors are, however, usually interested in the purpose for which the debtor who filed under Chapter 13 is now seeking credit, what his present income and expenses are, and what his ability to repay may be. They will probably be interested, as well, in the underlying circumstances that prompted the debtor to file under Chapter 13. They probably will be more receptive to granting credit to someone who got into financial trouble because of a personal misfortune he could not control, than to one of the classic cases who encountered disaster because of emotional or psychological shortcomings that he should have controlled.

These conditions also apply to Chapter 13 debtors who subsequently apply for VA- or FHA-guaranteed loans. Both of these agencies have declared policies that enable them to guarantee loans. They, too, will be concerned, however, that the debtor did not willfully obligate himself to pay several thousand dollars to creditors without the expectation and intention of paying back every dollar owed.

Effect on employment

A final concern of many who are considering bankruptcy or Chapter 13 is the effect they may have on present employment or their ability, in the future, to get a job. There are no easy answers to these questions. There are employers who will arbitrarily, as a matter of policy, dismiss an employee if it comes to their attention that a bankruptcy has been filed. This is particularly true in some sensitive occupations where financial problems are perceived as a sympton of instability, or might subject the employee to external pressures to betray confidences associated with his job. However, because no notification of the employer is required in either bankruptcy or Chapter 13, the odds are that the employer will not even be aware that these actions have been filed. Unless the bankrupt is a public figure, or there is some unusual or sensational element in the case, these cases usually escape the notice of the press.

Future employment opportunities are another matter. Many job applications require the applicant to reveal whether he has ever taken bankruptcy. Some employers, as a matter of policy, will refuse to employ him if the answer is "Yes." Others will simply be alerted by the response to probe him further to determine the circumstances surrounding the bankruptcy to determine whether it indicates a flaw in his character, or simply a misfortune that the applicant endured.

The important thing for the debtor who is considering legal alternatives, or seeking to avoid them, is to select an attorney who has a proven track record in handling personal financial problems. Debtor relief laws are a highly specialized area of legal practice, and the debtor should avoid consultation with a general practitioner or an attorney whose expertise lies in other fields. An attorney who is recommended by a friend or relative because he has ably handled another type of legal problem, may be totally

inadequate in a case of this kind. He may, however, be in a
position to refer you to another attorney who is a specialist
in the field.

How to find a lawyer

Finding the right lawyer can, in fact, be a vexing problem. Even within the field of debtor relief law there are
specialties within specialties. Some lawyers will not consider any approach except bankruptcy. Others are fully
committed to Chapter 13 and will not consider out-of-
court solutions or bankruptcy as alternatives. Consequently, the debtor must be extremely cautious to make
certain that he selects a lawyer who has the expertise and
the inclination to explain the available options and the
advantages and disadvantages that they present.

Unlike the purchase of a commodity, the quality of
legal representation cannot be determined by price. The
attorney who charges the highest fee is not necessarily the
one that will provide the most expert advice and efficient
service. On the other hand, those who advertise cut-rate
services often turn most of the work over to paralegals who
lack the detailed knowledge and experience that you are
entitled to expect. Some of the prepaid legal service plans
offer consumer bankruptcy and Chapter 13 services, but
none that I know of will assist with out-of-court workouts,
counseling, or debt management programs.

If you can't identify the appropriate attorney through
your own resources, such as inquiry among friends who
have filed bankruptcy or Chapter 13 or know others who
have, there are other avenues you can explore. You might,
for example, ask the clerk of the federal bankruptcy court
for the names of attorneys who file the largest volume of
Chapter 13 or bankruptcy cases. This will give you some
names with which to begin. A phone call to the Chapter
13 trustee or to the U.S. trustee's office may produce the

names of lawyers who regularly file cases under Chapter 13. (See list in Appendix A.) Be sure, though, when you talk to these lawyers, that you determine their willingness to file a bankruptcy instead, if that is a more appropriate thing to do.

Your local bar association undoubtedly maintains a list of lawyers specializing in various legal areas who are considered competent for referral. Or, if you are industrious, you might check the local bar association library for articles written by local attorneys that deal with bankruptcy and Chapter 13. An attorney who takes the time to write an article in this specialized field will probably be highly qualified, competent, and knowledgeable. Still another possibility is a call to the local bar association for the names of the attorneys serving on the bankruptcy and reorganization subcommittee. Usually, the most reputable and well-qualified attorneys are selected for service on these committees, and among them you may find the counselor you seek.

Arrange for interviews

Once you have gathered a list of potentially qualified attorneys, call them and arrange for interviews. Determine during that call, however, whether you will be charged for the initial visit. Determine, too, whether the attorney offers the whole range of solutions to his client's problem. When you have identified an attorney who meets those qualifications, and with whom you have the best rapport, put yourself in his hands and be completely open and honest in providing the information that he needs.

When you have selected your attorney and appear for your first formal meeting with him, be prepared to give him a complete breakdown of your personal financial situation. You should have a list of your fixed living expenses, estimated honestly and without any wishful thinking or concealment on your part. These items would include your rent or mortgage payments, utility costs, insurance costs, transportation costs, school expenses, expenditures for food, clothing, doctors and dentists, entertainment, and any other unusual obligations that you have which require a portion of your income. You should also have a list of all your installment obligations, including the monthly payment, balance due, amount in arrears, and the names, addresses, and telephone numbers of the creditors. Be prepared, as well, to identify those creditors who are being most persistent, or with whom an antagonistic relationship may have developed. Finally, be prepared to identify for your attorney all of the income you will receive from all sources during the ensuing year.

Be prepared

This kind of careful preparation will save your time and that of the attorney, for whom time is money. It will also enable him to deal more expeditiously with your problem. He will review your financial position, evaluate your creditors, and develop a plan of action. In some cases, on the basis of his experience, he may be able to zero in on one or two creditors who are actually the major cause of your problem. He may perceive that you have a defense against some of your debts because of violations of the Truth in Lending Act or unfair trade practices. If so, he may be able to resolve your problem by entering a defense against these claims, enabling you to fulfill your commitments on your other obligations.

Sometimes it is apparent that the debtor would be able to manage his affairs were it not for one large monthly obligation that is more than he can handle. The attorney may determine that if the debtor is willing to tighten his belt and return some collateral in order to dispose of the back-breaking payment, he may be able to manage his affairs again. The attorney may take responsibility for negotiating the return of the security and wiping out the balance.

There are other situations in which it becomes clear to the attorney that the financial problems stem from a temporary loss of income and will disappear when that income is restored. Perhaps the husband and wife have both been employed and one of them has been without income temporarily because of an injury or some other cause. Things should return to normal within a short period of time.

Drastic measures, such as Chapter 13 or bankruptcy, are certainly not called for in situations such as this. More appropriately, the attorney can contact the creditors and arrange for a moratorium of payment for the period until the debtor's income returns to the normal level.

In situations such as these, the resolution of the debtor's problems is relatively simple, provided it is clear that after negotiating the arrangements, the debtor can consistently meet his monthly obligations as contracted. If not, the attorney should then proceed to the more drastic options already described.

6

Chapter 13: Neglected alternative to bankruptcy

Before Joe and Jan visited the attorney who had been recommended to them, they reviewed their financial situation carefully. They went over their canceled checks and bills for the past year and made the best estimate they could, on a monthly basis, of what it cost them to live. Then they listed all of their outstanding obligations, recording the name, address, and telephone number of the creditor, the balance owed, the monthly payment required, and the amount of arrears. Having done that they felt they were in a position to talk knowledgeably with the attorney about their financial situation.

"We're desperate," Joe confessed to the lawyer as they faced him across his desk. "Since Jan had to quit working we simply haven't been able to keep up with our bills. Our monthly expenses exceed my income, so there is no way we can pay them all. Now one of our creditors has exercised a wage assignment, my boss is upset, and I'm afraid that if a couple more of our creditors slap us with garnishments, I'll lose my job. Then I don't know what we will do."

Joe handed their financial statement to the attorney. He studied it for a few minutes, asked a few questions, and made a few calculations.

"I can see why you're concerned," the attorney said, "but it may make you feel better to know that I see many people every day who are in much worse shape. Nevertheless, I'm afraid you're in so deep and have waited so long to try to correct the situation that any kind of voluntary debt reduction plan is out of the question. You probably won't have to file bankruptcy, but I think you will want to seek the protection of the U.S. District Court under Chapter 13."

Basics of Chapter 13

Joe and Jan looked at each other, obviously puzzled, and the lawyer realized that they didn't know what he was talking about. "Don't be alarmed," he reassured them, taking a couple of printed folders from his desk drawer. "Chapter 13 is a legal procedure under the bankruptcy act that may be the solution to all of your financial problems. Here's a simple explanation prepared by the trustee appointed by the U.S. District Court. It's a little out of date, because Chapter 13 is no longer restricted to wage earners, but it is a good summary of what Chapter 13 is all about."

Joe and Jan took the folders and began to read:

The Chapter 13 Wage Earner Law

The Chapter 13 Wage Earner Plan is a federal law enacted by the U.S. Congress to help people who find themselves in

financial difficulty and unable to pay their debts. The Wage
Earner Law provides a way for financially overburdened
wage earners to pay all debts and avoid the embarrassment
of bankruptcy. The Wage Earner Law allows the employee
to pay his debts through reduced payments budgeted to his
income and living expenses—payments he can afford.

All payments by the wage earner are made to the court-
appointed trustee for Chapter 13 Wage Earner Plans. An
officer of the U.S. District Court, the trustee administers all
Wage Earner Plans in his district, disbursing the wage
earner's payments to creditors and helping with the day to
day problems that may arise between debtors and creditors,
under the supervision of a U.S. District Court bankruptcy
judge. Fees for a Wage Earner Plan are court-controlled. All
costs including attorney's and trustee's fees are included in
the regular payments.

Joe looked up from the pamphlet and asked: "You mean
we can get a federal court trustee to help us manage our
bill payments and get our finances squared away without
going bankrupt?"

"That's right," the attorney replied, "but that's not all
the court will do for you. Read on."

Joe turned his attention back to the pamphlet and
continued reading:

How Chapter 13 protects the wage earner

13 Stops Wage Assignments
and Harassment by Creditors

The salaried employee who finds his job in jeopardy
because of wage assignments and creditor harassment can
gain the protection of the U.S. District Court by filing a
Wage Earner Plan.

An automatic stay order comes into effect immediately
upon filing a Chapter 13 petition that prohibits all creditors
from contacting a wage earner's employer and stops all

legal action such as wage assignments and wage deduction orders. Further, the order prohibits all creditors from trying to collect from the wage earner by telephone, writing, dunning or harassing him, or by instituting lawsuits against him. In short, the wage earner and his employer are immediately relieved of any collection contact from creditors. The creditors instead contact the trustee or the debtor's attorney.

13 Stops Service Charges, Late Charges, and, in Most Cases, Interest

The restraining order also stops all service charges, late charges, and usually, interest from accruing. The wage earner often saves more by elimination of these charges and interest than the total cost to him of the Wage Earner Plan.

13 Stops Repossessions

Unlike bankruptcy, the Wage Earner Law allows the debtor to retain possession of all personal property—automobiles, appliances, furniture, jewelry, and furs.

13 Protects Equity and Savings

The Wage Earner Law also protects equity in real estate holdings, stocks and bonds, savings accounts, and insurance policies.

13 Rejects Invalid Claims

The court may hold hearings to consider the validity of all creditor claims. It rules on disputed bills and can deny all claims that are unfair or unfounded.

When Joe finished reading his face was a study in perplexity and astonishment.

"I can't believe it," he said. "Does this mean that we could have avoided all the abuse and embarrassment we've been subjected to, and paid our bills at a rate we could afford, simply by filing a Chapter 13 plan?"

The lawyer smiled again. "Yes, if you're eligible and we can develop a plan that is acceptable to the court, that's exactly what I mean."

"But what about my employer," Joe asked, still searching for the Catch 22. "Won't this get me in trouble with him?"

"On the contrary," the attorney assured him. "You've already had a wage assignment filed against you which your employer will have to execute. This is a costly nuisance for him and, as you already have learned, he isn't happy about it. If the court confirms your plan under Chapter 13 the wage assignment will not be honored by the employer. But that's not all. Your other creditors won't be able to bother your employer, either, nor will they be able to bother you. That's important to your employer, because he obviously regards you as a valued employee or he wouldn't have bothered to send you to me. After you've filed and the wage assignment has been stopped, he won't have to worry that you may switch jobs in order to escape it. More important, he can pretty well expect that your morale and productivity will be improved because your financial worries will be off your mind.

Avoiding stigma of bankruptcy

"There's another less tangible benefit, too," the lawyer continued. "It's obvious from what you've told me that you are honest, sincere people who really want to pay your bills. Chapter 13 will enable you to do that, and avoid the stigma of bankruptcy. You'll feel better knowing that you have faced up to your responsibilities, and your creditors will be better off, too. If you declared bankruptcy all of your assets would be exempt, and your creditors wouldn't get a dime. When you file your plan under Chapter 13, they will receive regular payments from the trustee, and ultimately much or all of what you now owe them will be paid. As a matter of fact, creditors are always sure to get more money under a Chapter 13 plan than they would have in a bankruptcy liquidation. That is a major condition precedent to confirmation of the Chapter 13 plan.

"I think you'll agree from what I've told you that Chapter 13 is a truly remarkable solution to credit problems. If you seek protection under Chapter 13, everyone wins; if you are discharged in bankruptcy, nobody does."

7

Eligibility to file under Chapter 13

When their lawyer told them that more than two hundred thousand bankruptcy cases had been filed in 1978, compared with about thirty thousand cases filed under Chapter 13, Joe and Jan were surprised.

"Are you sure we're eligible to file a plan under Chapter 13?" Jan asked. "It must be difficult to qualify for Chapter 13 because otherwise, if it is as desirable a remedy as you say it is, I should think those numbers would be the other way around."

"Not so at all," the attorney assured her. "Many of those who filed bankruptcy could have filed under Chapter 13. They didn't do so for three reasons. First, many attorneys are unfamiliar with Chapter 13, so their clients aren't informed about it. Other lawyers don't recommend Chapter 13 to their clients because they feel, compared to bank-

ruptcy, that they get too small a fee for too much work.
Finally, prior to the enactment of the Bankruptcy Reform
Act of 1978, no provision had been made in many jurisdictions to administer Chapter 13 cases. Because no mechanism was available, few if any Chapter 13 cases were filed.
This has been greatly improved under the new act. It
provides for the appointment of a U.S. trustee in 17
districts. He will administer Chapter 13 cases if there is no
standing trustee already in existence. With this mechanism
in place in 17 districts with substantial populations, I'm
sure we'll see a huge increase in Chapter 13 filings in the
years ahead."

No limit on income

The attorney also explained that Chapter 13 had originally been limited to wage earners whose income did not
exceed $3,000 a year. Later, he said, the limit was raised to
$5,000, and finally the income ceiling had been removed
entirely, so Joe's income did not preclude their filing a
plan. Under the 1978 reform act, he continued, the provisions had been broadened even further. Chapter 13 protection was extended to any individual with a regular income
from a business or profession who owes less than $100,000
in noncontingent liquidated unsecured debts and less than
$350,000 in noncontingent liquidated secured obligations.

The lawyer pointed out that Chapter 13 and, in fact, the
bankruptcy act itself was not devised to aid the poor.
Rather, it was intended to help those in middle and upper
income brackets who had something to lose. Its purpose is
to make it possible for individuals who are under pressure
because of financial problems to liquidate their debts in an
orderly manner. The size of their income is immaterial, so
long as the income is regular and sufficient to support an
orderly Chapter 13 repayment plan within the time period
allowed. Theoretically, an individual earning one hundred

thousand dollars a year or more, and with substantial material assets, could file under Chapter 13 if he was experiencing cash flow problems that made it impossible for him to handle his monthly payment obligations on a current basis. He would, of course, have to meet the criteria included in the bankruptcy act and propose a plan that was acceptable to the court.

He would have to propose a plan in which his creditors received at least as much as they would receive in a bankruptcy liquidation. If the value of his nonexempt assets exceeded his debts, he would have to propose a plan under which he would pay 100 percent of what he owed his creditors. He would also have to demonstrate that he needed relief. He might do this by demonstrating that, because of a depressed stock or real estate market, a liquidation would force him to take a substantial loss on stocks or real property.

8

Procedures under Chapter 13

The attorney then explained to Joe and Jan that in most Chapter 13 cases a plan is proposed to the court offering to pay all creditors in full over an extended period of time. Until October 1, 1979, this period was generally three years, but under the new act, with the approval of the judge, the period can be as long as five years.

Debtors whose income is insufficient to repay their obligations in full within the period of the plan can offer a composition plan. They propose to pay the percentage of their unsecured debts that is feasible within the income that is available to them during the three- to five-year time period that the law allows.

The couple learned that composition plans had been infrequently used under the old bankruptcy act because, if the wage earner found himself in trouble again, he would not be eligible to file bankruptcy for six full years from the date of filing the old plan. Under the new act, if the debtor repaid 70 percent of his debts under the plan, he remains eligible to declare bankruptcy at any time. If he has not paid 70 percent of his debts under a prior composition plan, the debtor cannot file for bankruptcy for six years, but it appears that he is still eligible to file another Chapter 13 at any time. This change, the lawyer said, would probably encourage a large increase in composition plans.

Be sure figures are accurate

The attorney questioned Joe and Jan closely about the figures they had presented to him, urging them to make certain that they were not understating the sum required for fixed living expenses, and that they had not overlooked any creditors who should be included in the plan. When he had satisfied himself that they had presented an accurate statement of their financial requirements, he turned to a desk calculator and began punching buttons. When he had finished he said:

"It appears, after covering your fixed living expenses, that you have a surplus of $410 a month which could be used to repay your creditors under your plan. Your obligations total $12,000, so you could repay all of your creditors in a three-year period with payments of $333 per month. Add 10 percent to that for the cost of administration and trustee's fees and we get a total of a little under $370 a month. That's a little tight, but you'll have $40 a month left over for unusual expenses, and you'll be out of debt in three years' time. You'll be able to pay everyone in full without even filing a composition plan.

"In some cases I'd be concerned about signing a debtor up for a plan that had so little room for error, but you seem to have learned your lesson. I believe you are really willing to adhere to a tight budget and refrain from making any credit purchases for the duration of the plan. Besides, although it would be a mistake to count on it, if Jan goes back to work you'll have much more flexibility. You'll be able to put her income in the bank and start building a fund for emergencies.

"Once the proposed petition and plan is filed with the court," the lawyer promised, "your creditors will automatically be stayed from contacting you or your employer further in any way. The wage assignment will be ineffective, which will make your boss happy and will give you the opportunity to concentrate on doing your job so that you can make your monthly payments to the trustee. He'll disburse the funds in your behalf, and your creditors, from then on, will deal with him, not with you."

Jan smiled at that thought, but then a frown darkened her face.

"It sounds great," she said. "You can't imagine what a relief it would be to be rid of all those threatening phone calls, to know that we can keep the car, and that Joe won't be in danger of losing his job. But what about the cost? We already owe so much, I wonder if we can really afford to pay that 10 percent to the trustee. And what about the court costs and the fee that you're going to charge?"

"You can't afford not to pay it," the lawyer replied. "Unless you want to go through bankruptcy, you really don't have any other choice. But there's a more positive answer than that. Remember that pamphlet you read? Right now you're paying about 18 percent in interest or finance charges on almost everything you owe. Once you file under Chapter 13, all of those charges stop. Sure, you'll be paying 10 percent to the trustee on the amount he disburses, but you'll be saving the 18 percent you're paying in finance charges on the total balance that you owe. Dollar-wise you'll be better off than you would have been if your income had enabled you to pay off your debts as originally agreed.

"As for the other costs," he continued, "they're really nominal as compared to the problem you've got and the sums you already owe. The filing fee under the new act is $60 and my fee, which must be approved by the court, will be $600. But you don't have to come up with all that money in advance. Payment can be included as part of the plan."

Procedure

"But how long does it take?" Joe asked. "We're under an awful lot of pressure, and there's my boss to worry about. Legal matters always seem to drag on and on, and I'm afraid something disastrous will happen before the court gets around to straightening things out."

"That's not the case with Chapter 13," the lawyer assured him. "I'll prepare the plan and the necessary legal documents for your signatures. I think you and Jan should file jointly, so that her income is not in jeopardy if she goes back to work. We can probably get all of this done and file it within 24 hours. Once the plan is filed your creditors will automatically be stayed from proceeding further against you. As a courtesy, I'll notify them that the Chapter 13 has been filed, and soon thereafter each of them will receive a copy of the plan and a claim form, along with a notice that tells them the date of the first meeting of creditors."

"What happens at the meeting?" Jan asked.

"This is the day you go to court with me for a meeting with your creditors and the trustee. It is probably the only time you will have to appear,* and the procedure is quite informal. The trustee may ask you a few questions, but most of the information he needs is already provided in

---

*The procedure will vary from district to district. In some, debtors may also have to appear for confirmation and discharge.

the plan. The trustee may commend you for choosing Chapter 13 rather than a bankruptcy, and will probably remind you of the importance of making your payments to him on time. He'll probably tell you that he expects you to begin making payments right away.

"It's probable that most of your creditors won't even appear at the meeting, and it isn't likely that any questions will be raised by those who do. The whole procedure usually takes only a few minutes. All that remains is for the trustee to have the plan approved by the court. That's almost automatic, because the court must approve the plan if you have met six conditions that are spelled out in the act. This, incidentally, is a substantial change from the old law. In past years it was necessary to secure the acceptance of the plan by a majority of your creditors before the plan could be confirmed. If you meet the tests of the bankruptcy reform act, the creditors no longer have a voice in the matter."

The attorney informed the couple that after confirmation of their plan, creditors would have six months in which to file their claims. If they failed to do so within that period, the debt would be discharged. He told them not to be surprised if many of their creditors failed to file. In Chicago, he said, the standing trustee had advised him that about 40 percent of creditors failed to file their claims, and the debts were discharged. This made it possible for the trustee to liquidate the remaining obligations in a shorter period of time than contemplated in the plan.

"But why would any of the creditors fail to file?" Jan asked. "Certainly they all want to be paid."

"There's no clear answer to that question," the attorney replied, "but I have some notions about it. I think some of them fail to file because of sloppy administration in their own office. The papers come in and are put aside or mislaid by an employee who doesn't know what they mean. But more often, I suspect, the creditor assumes that the debtor has filed a bankruptcy petition, and doesn't realize that the filing is under Chapter 13. That's because in most jurisdictions all cases filed under the bankruptcy act are numbered in order, with no distinction shown between straight bankruptcy and Chapter 13."

The attorney concluded the meeting by advising them that there is also a provision of Chapter 13 that would protect them in the event that any objectionable claims were filed. Approximately 60 days after the first meeting he would check the claims that had been filed by creditors, and if any were not in their schedule, or were for amounts greater than scheduled, he would object to them. In that event the court would set a date for a hearing to determine the validity of the claims.

Joe and Jan, eagerly anticipating a life free from harassment, worry, and fear, happily agreed to have the attorney file the plan.

9

The Bankruptcy Reform
Act of 1978

Joe and Jan were the beneficiaries of an Act of Congress
that was carefully designed to provide troubled debtors
with a clean financial slate, so they can begin life anew
unburdened by past misfortunes or mistakes. The Bankruptcy Reform Act of 1978, which became effective on
October 1, 1979, is the first major revision of federal bankruptcy laws since 1938. It was the result of a legislative
process that began with the establishment of a commission
on bankruptcy laws in 1970. The commission's report to
the Congress on July 30, 1973, was followed by a succes-
sion of legislative proposals that meandered through the
two houses until the much-amended reform act finally was
enacted in October 1978. It is clear from the legislative
history that most of the changes in the act were made to
correct inequities or inadequacies of the old law that

sometimes denied debtors the "fresh start" it was supposed to provide.

The revision was sorely needed because, after the passage of 40 years, the 1938 act was no longer relevant to the needs of the times. That act dealt primarily with business bankruptcies, rather than consumer problems, because consumer bankruptcies were not a significant factor at the time of its enactment. Consequently, it did not provide adequate relief for the consumer debtor in an era in which consumer credit has expanded so enormously.

The Congress was aware, in fact, that in many cases Chapter 13 of the old law actually discourages debtors from using it. In many jurisdictions no mechanism had been established to enable debtors to employ Chapter 13. In others the act was badly administered, and in many cases debtors attempting to pay their creditors under its provisions were inadequately supervised. The new act was intended to cure the perceived inadequacies of the old Chapter 13, and of the bankruptcy provisions of the act, as well.

Chapter 13 provides a structure that enables an individual to develop and carry out a plan for the repayment of creditors over an extended period of time. It is intended to relieve the debtor of both direct and indirect creditor pressure and harassment, which tend to impair the quality of his work performance, threaten his marriage, and often make it more difficult for him to manage his financial affairs. Unlike a liquidation under Chapter 7 of the act, Chapter 13 allows the debtor to retain his property and protect his assets by agreeing to repay his creditors, under court supervision, in a specified period of time. Thus he is able to support himself and his dependents in an adequate manner while simultaneously retiring his debts. It is also assumed that the debtor who successfully completes a Chapter 13 plan will emerge with less damage to his personal and credit reputation because he chose to pay his debts, rather than resorting to bankruptcy to wipe them out. In short, by opting for Chapter 13 rather than liquidation, he demonstrates responsible citizenship.

The old act limited the use of Chapter 13 to "wage earners," defined as individuals "whose principal income is derived from wages, salary or commissions." That is why, in the pamphlet that Joe and Jan read, it was referred to as "the wage earner plan." The new act extends the protection of Chapter 13 to professional people and small businessmen who have a regular income from sources other than wages and commissions. The only limitations are these: Chapter 13 is not available to a stock broker or a commodity broker, and the total of the debtor's obligations on the date of filing must be less than $100,000 in noncontingent liquidated unsecured debts, and less than $350,000 in noncontingent liquidated secured obligations. This maximum does not apply to the wage earner, who remains eligible to file under Chapter 13 regardless of the amount he owes.

Plan is completely voluntary

As was the case under the prior law, Chapter 13 remains completely voluntary. The debtor has the exclusive right to propose a repayment plan, and cannot be forced by his creditors into a plan that he does not wish to accept. Proposals for involuntary filing were firmly rejected by the Congress for two major reasons. First, such a provision could result in situations in which debtors were forced to work for the benefit of their creditors, a result that might be in conflict with the Thirteenth Amendment, the constitutional prohibition against involuntary servitude. Moreover, experience under the old Chapter 13 had indicated that success is likely only with a willing and cooperative debtor. Thus, it appeared likely that if a debtor were forced into a plan, it would probably fail.

The new act also remedies a defect that was responsible for the collapse of many plans under the old Chapter 13. It continues the automatic stay action, which prevents creditors from moving against debtors once they have filed a plan, but it also extends that protection to those who have cosigned notes with the debtor. Formerly, creditors who were prohibited from acting against the debtor often transferred their attention to those who had cosigned his notes. They can no longer do this in consumer debt cases, but the prohibition does not apply to debts incurred in the ordinary course of business, or if the case was closed, dismissed, or converted to another chapter.

The new act also expands the group of debtors who may avail themselves of Chapter 13 by extending the time for completion of a plan. The old act extending the time for completion of a plan. The old act generally required that the debtor present a plan within his available income, that could be completed in three years. A debtor with secured debts which exceeded the income available to pay them in that length of time was ineligible to file under Chapter 13, except in those rare instances when the court was willing to approve a longer plan.

Under the reform act, if the debtor's surplus income is not sufficient to complete the plan in 36 monthly payments, the act permits the court to approve a plan of up to, but no more than, five years. In many cases, with two years of additional income to apply to them, the secured debts could be paid, and the debtor would be eligible to file a plan. To make things still easier for the debtor, the new act also permits payment of claims from a combination of future income and liquidation of some of the debtor's property.

The trustee is the principal actor

The trustee is really the man in charge, as an agent of

the court, in a Chapter 13 case. The new act has preserved the concept of the standing trustee, which had proved to be relatively successful under the prior law.

The new act introduces, for the first time, the concept of a United States trustee who will act in cases instituted under its provisions. It provides that the attorney general shall appoint one U.S. trustee for each of the following districts: 1) the district of Maine, New Hampshire, Massachusetts, and Rhode Island; 2) the southern district of New York; 3) the district of Delaware and New Jersey; 4) the eastern district of Virginia and the District of Columbia; 5) the northern district of Alabama; 6) the northern district of Texas; 7) the northern district of Illinois; 8) the district of Minnesota, North and South Dakota; 9) the central district of California; and 10) the district of Colorado and Kansas.

The concept of the U.S. trustee is an experimental one, undertaken as a pilot project. It will expire in 1984, under a "sunset" provision, unless the Congress takes further action to extend it. It should significantly effect the administration of Chapter 13 cases because one of the new trustee's duties is to supervise the administration of cases under this chapter. The act also provides that if the number of cases filed under Chapter 13 in any district warrants it, the U.S. trustee of the district, with the approval of the attorney general, may appoint one or more persons to serve as standing trustees. The effect of these provisions will be to make a facility for handling Chapter 13 cases available in some jurisdictions where none was available in the past.

Creditor approval no longer required

Under the old Chapter 13, if a majority of the creditors—in both number and dollar amounts of outstanding debts—failed to accept the plan, it could not be confirmed by the court. Many a debtor was driven to bankruptcy because his creditors would not go along with his plan.

The elimination of this requirement is one of the most significant changes in the new law. It simply requires a determination that the plan is in the best interests of the creditors: that they will receive at least as much money under the Chapter 13 as they would have received if the debtor's assets were liquidated in bankruptcy. This determination is made by calculating the value of the *nonexempt* assets of the debtor and comparing that figure with the sum that he proposes to pay under the plan. Because the exemptions the debtor may claim under the new act have been liberalized so generously, the odds are that in most cases the debtor will be able to propose repayment greater than the nonexempt value of the estate. This will probably be true even under plans proposing that the debtor pay as little as 10 percent of his unsecured debts. The unsecured creditors no longer have any right to vote on the plan.

The secured creditor, under the new act, also has very little power to prevent the plan from being confirmed by the court. If he refuses to accept a plan which extends the period during which he will be paid, the court can still confirm if the debtor elects to return the property. If the debtor wishes to keep the property, the court can allow the creditor to retain a lien securing his claim, but still confirm the plan provided the debtor proposes to pay for it under the plan. However, the debtor is not required to repay the full amount owed to the secured creditor. He must only make payments equal to the value of the security, plus the same percentage of the remaining balance that he is paying to his other unsecured creditors.

The important word here is *value*. Let's assume that John and Mary bought some furniture from one of the high pressure credit furniture stores that advertise on TV. They were lured to the store by a promise that the store could furnish three rooms for $239, but fell victims to a bait and switch routine, and ended up spending three thousand bucks.

When John and Mary fall upon evil times, the friendly furniture merchant is the first vulture to land on their backs. They are finally forced to file a plan under Chapter 13. Although the furniture merchant has a lien on their furniture, and they still owe him $2,400, they don't have to pay that much. They need only agree to pay the current value of the furniture, which was such junk in the first place that it wouldn't sell for more than a couple of hundred dollars. They would agree to pay the two hundred dollar value under the plan. The remaining $2,200 of their obligation to the furniture store would be treated as an unsecured debt. If the plan was a composition plan which proposed paying 10 percent to unsecured creditors, they would pay the merchant 10 percent of the $2,200 balance, or $220. Added to the $200 payment on the secured portion of the debt, this would total $440. That is what the furniture dealer would get, instead of the $2,400 remaining on their note.

Don't feel sorry for the furniture merchant. He is less considerate of every customer who walks into his store. More important, he would have no power to keep the court from confirming the plan. If John and Mary complete the plan, the entire debt will be discharged. This has become known as the "cram down" provision, presumably because it is one on which many secured creditors will choke.

Conditions that must be met

The new act also provides that if certain conditions are met, the court itself has no power to refuse to confirm a plan under Chapter 13. It provides that the court *shall* confirm a plan if:

1. The plan complies with the provisions of Chapter 13 and any applicable provisions of the remainder of the act.
2. The required fees have been paid.
3. The plan has been proposed in good faith and not by any means forbidden by law.
4. The value, as of the effective date of the plan, of property to be distributed under the plan on account of each allowed unsecured claim is not less than the amount that would be paid in a bankruptcy liquidation.
5. With respect to each allowed secured claim provided for by the plan,
   (a) the holder of the claim has accepted the plan;
   (b) the plan provides that the holder of the claim will retain a lien securing it, and be paid the *value,* as of the effective date of the plan, to be distributed to him during the plan; or
   (c) the debtor surrenders the property securing the claim; and
6. The debtor will be able to make all payments under the plan and to comply with the plan.

Provisions regarding real property

Debtors who have obligations that extend for a period longer than the plan, such as a home mortgage, can make payments on schedule as part of the plan, and then continue the payments after completion of the plan. If the mortgage is in default at the time of filing, provision can be made to cure the default within the period of the plan. Meanwhile, the mortgagor is stayed from foreclosing on the property so long as the debtor is meeting the provisions of the plan.

Debtors whose obligations include unpaid income taxes can't escape them, but they also may benefit from Chapter 13. If you fail to pay your taxes, the Internal Revenue

Service has the right to file a lien against your wages and take a good portion of your paycheck until the taxes are paid in full. The automatic stay under Chapter 13 stops federal wage liens, and the IRS, as a general rule, will file a claim to be paid under the debtor's plan.

If a debtor, after confirmation of his plan, finds that for reasons beyond his control, he cannot make the payments to which he is committed, he can request modification of the plan. The court, in these cases, can grant a reduction of payments or an extension of time to make it feasible for the debtor to complete the plan. On the other hand, the court is also permitted to revoke a confirmation order that has been procured by fraud.

Court can grant hardship discharge

The former Chapter 13 allowed the court to grant a hardship discharge if the plan had not been completed during the three-year period after confirmation. The new law liberalizes this provision by allowing a hardship discharge at any time after confirmation of the plan. However, three conditions must be met: 1) the debtor's failure to complete payments must be due to circumstances for which he could not justly be held accountable; 2) the debtor must have paid at least liquidation value determined as of the effective date of the plan; and 3) it must be shown that modification of the plan to permit its completion is not feasible.

Let's say Jack and Jill filed a composition plan under Chapter 13 and it was confirmed by the court. Six months later Jack fell down the hill, suffering an injury that forced him to take a disability retirement. His retirement pay was barely enough to live on, so he could no longer make the payments to the trustee. Jack would be eligible to file for a hardship discharge without completing the plan.

As in the old law, the new act permits the court to order that the plan payment be deducted by the debtor's employer and mailed to the trustee. This removes any temptation from the debtor to spend the money required for the plan, instead of turning it over to the trustee. The debtor may, however, elect to receive his full paycheck and make his own payments to the trustee.

In the event of loss of employment or some other misfortune that makes it impossible for the debtor to carry out his commitments under the plan, the new act gives the debtor the right to convert to a straight bankruptcy at any time. Waiver of this right is made unenforceable. In addition, for cause shown, the court now has the power to convert a Chapter 13 case to a straight bankruptcy under Chapter 7, or to dismiss the case. This could happen, for example, if the debtor fell behind in his plan because he failed to make the required payments to the trustee.

10

A hypothetical case under Chapter 13

After passage of the Bankruptcy Reform Act, a group of bankruptcy judges, attending seminars in Atlanta and Salt Lake City, were entertained by the presentation of a hypothetical action brought under the new Chapter 13. The details of the case were grossly exaggerated for emphasis, but the script provides a dramatic example of the extent to which debtors may benefit from the new provisions, or even abuse them if they choose to.

A Chapter 13 drama

CAST:

John Doe, a swinging, fun loving, hospitable, generous, GS 16 government employee who cannot stay out of debt. Doe remains offstage throughout.

Hughes, Doe's most recent attorney.

Kline, the bankruptcy judge.

Blinn, attorney for GMAC, American Express, and GMAC employee Peter Dare.

Gandy, attorney for Citizens and Southern Bank.

Sonny Day, bank employee.

Time: 9 A.M. October 3, 1979.

Scene: Judge Kline's chambers. The judge and the three attorneys are seated around the desk. Doe's Chapter 13 petition is on the desk. Among other things, the petition reveals:

Doe's income is $45,000 a year.

He has no dependents.

He resides in a furnished apartment two blocks from his office.

His only assets, other than wearing apparel, are:

Earned but unpaid salary	$1,000
1978 Corvette automobile in poor condition	5,000
Wine cellar	6,000
Sailboat	5,000
	$17,000

He received a discharge in bankruptcy cases filed in 1970 and 1977.

His creditors are:

Internal Revenue Service, 1978 taxes	$10,000
GMAC, secured by Corvette	10,000
C & S Bank, secured by sailboat	10,000
C & S Bank, unsecured loan obtained by an admittedly false financial statement	10,000

Peter Dare, personal injury judgment (Injury
    occurred when Dare, attempting
    repossession, was struck by Doe's car, Doe
    being intoxicated and angry at the time.
    Doe meant only to frighten Dare but broke
    both of his legs.)   20,000

Sonny Day, battery judgment (Day phoned Doe
    at the office once too often; Doe went to the
    bank and broke Day's jaw.)   20,000

American Express (wine, women, song, travel)   20,000

Doe's plan provides that:

1. IRS receive $400 monthly until $10,000 is paid.
2. GMAC and C&S each receive $200 monthly until they
   are paid $5,000 each on their secured claims.
3. Nothing be paid on nonpriority unsecured claims.

JUDGE KLINE: I must say this is an extraordinary case,
    gentlemen.

GANDY: We appreciate your seeing us at this time. John
    Blinn and I believe this petition is a fraud on the
    court, completely void of good faith and should not
    be tolerated by you for one more hour.

BLINN: Exactly, judge. The only reason Doe filed was to
    frustrate our repossession team. We've been working
    night and day for six months trying to find his car,
    and we finally located it in his girl friend's garage.

KLINE: I suppose that's not too friendly of Doe, but can I
    kick his case out of court just because he wants to
    block repossession? If so, I would have to dismiss half
    of all chapter cases.

GANDY: Maybe not on that ground alone, judge, but
    because it is part of the whole sordid mess.

HUGHES: Easy now! What's so sordid?

BLINN: First off, judge, he doesn't propose to pay unsecured creditors a nickel. That in itself proves the plan
is not in good faith. The whole point of Chapter 13 is
to pay creditors out of future earnings.

KLINE: Makes sense. What do you say to that?

HUGHES: We are paying creditors out of future earnings—
the taxes and the car and the boat. But even if we
weren't, Sec. 1322(a) (1) only requires use of earnings
in a plan "as is necessary for its execution."

GANDY: I agree with Blinn. Sec. 1322(b) (8) speaks of
payment "of all or any part of a claim" and you're not
paying any part of the unsecured claims. The plan's a
fraud and the petition's a fraud.

HUGHES: Judge, the section Gandy is referring to is per-
missive, it is not mandatory.

KLINE: Perhaps so, but it indicates to me that Congress
intended at least part payment on each claim.

HUGHES: If that's true, I can amend the plan to pay $1 on
each unsecured claim.

BLINN: See, judge. It's just a game with him. I tell you,
Hughes and Doe are trying to make a fool of you.

KLINE: Now, now, counsel. Let's not get personal. (to
Hughes): What kind of a fool do you think I am?

HUGHES: I apologize if that sounded like an insult, but I
am serious. If $1 is not enough, what is? How about 1
percent, 5 percent, 10 percent, 25 percent of each
unsecured claim? There's nothing in the code to guide
us. Certainly, there is no grant of discretion to the
court.

GANDY: Let's pass that, judge. There are so many reasons
why this plan can't make it. For sure, Hughes can't
get the unsecured creditors to accept this plan and the
secured creditors will fight to the Supreme Court.

KLINE: I read some place that unsecured creditors don't
vote on the plan.

HUGHES: There you go, a real scholar.

BLINN: That may not be correct. It is true that, unlike Chapter 13 under the act and Chapter 11 under the code, there is no provision for voting. However, we know that the rules apply to the code unless it is inconsistent, and the rules governing voting are not inconsistent because the code does not prohibit voting.

HUGHES: Now who's ridiculous?

BLINN: Wait a minute. Take a look at Sec. 1327(a)—the confirmed plan binds a creditor whether he has accepted or rejected the plan. This may mean that Congress contemplated voting by unsecured creditors.

HUGHES: I don't think so. That's just a reference to secured creditors. See Sec. 1325(a) (5) (A).

KLINE: This is unproductive. Let's move on.

GANDY: Even if Doe gets to a confirmation hearing, he can't get past it because of his straight bankruptcy discharge in 1977. You can't confirm a composition plan if the debtor would be denied a discharge under Sec. 727. That's horn-book law.

KLINE: Dean, I've been looking at Sec. 1325 and I don't find any requirement that the court must find the debtor would not be denied a discharge under Chapter 7.

BLINN: Wow!

GANDY: That must be a mistake. Do you mean that if Doe refused to obey a lawful order of this court, or committed a bankruptcy crime, or did any of the reprehensible things that would bar discharge, Judge Kline could still confirm this miserable plan?

HUGHES: I don't mean anything; I'm just trying to earn a living. But to answer your question, I think the judge not only could confirm but must confirm. Sec. 1325 says the court *shall* confirm if various facts are found and eligibility for discharge is not one of them.

BLINN: I grant that a literal reading of Sec. 1325 supports

Hughes, but Congress could not have meant to permit confirmation of what amounts to a no-asset plan for general creditors under circumstances that would have been a bar to discharge if the debtor chose Chapter 7 instead of Chapter 13.

HUGHES: Of course it could. Chapter 13 confirmations are no different from Chapter 11 confirmations in this regard.

GANDY: You're wrong there. The difference is that we creditors can reject a Chapter 11 plan and even propose one of our own.

KLINE: Whatever Congress meant, I'm still bound by what it said. Let's move on to something more productive.

BLINN: I don't think you can confirm this plan, judge, because it obviously is not in good faith as required by Sec. 1325(a) (3) and I'm not sure Hughes can satisfy you as to Sec. 1325(a) (4).

GANDY: I agree. This is as clear a case of bad faith as I've seen.

HUGHES: Good faith has a narrow meaning, such as the debtor truly believing his plan is feasible. It cannot mean that the judge can apply his values on a plan that complies in all respects with statutory law.

KLINE: I'm inclined to agree. The good faith element existed under the act and is part of Chapter 11. I don't think it permits me to rule contrary to the plain language of the code just because I may disagree with what Congress has done.

HUGHES: Judge, you impress me as a Supreme Court candidate.

BLINN: Well, what about the "best interest" test? Sec. 1325(a) (4) says you don't confirm unless unsecured creditors receive as much under the plan as they would under Chapter 7. The language is "not less than."

HUGHES: That's easy. The zero payout under the plan is not less than the zero payout in straight bankruptcy.

GANDY: Perhaps so, but who has the burden of proving there would be nothing for creditors in Chapter 7? The schedules show $17,000 in assets.

HUGHES: I can make out a *prima facie* case that the sailboat and auto are oversecured and the balance of the assets would be exempt under the federal alternative. As I see it, the burden is then on you to prove otherwise.

GANDY: I doubt that, but I'd like an explanation of how you get off paying my client only $5,000 on the boat. We've got a secured claim for $10,000.

BLINN: Let me take this one. I've concluded, regretfully, that Hughes is correct. The Chapter 13 cram down— Sec. 1325(a) (5) (B)—only requires payment of the value of the allowed amount of the secured claim. Sec. 506(a) tells us what the allowed amount of a secured claim is: the value of the creditor's interest in the property. In other words, the value of the collateral.

KLINE: Gentlemen, we seem to be spinning our wheels. Is there anything we can accomplish this morning?

GANDY: Maybe not. It looks like he can cram this damn plan down our throats, but it may not be so bad after all. Two of my claims are nondischargeable. Doe's going to have to take care of them one way or another.

BLINN: I'm with you. He can't wipe out Dare's judgment. The judge found Doe's action to be willful, wanton, malicious, and gross negligence of the worst kind. And he's been defrauding American Express for years.

KLINE: That's right, Hughes. It looks like you're going to have to make your peace. You concede you couldn't win a false financial statement case against the bank, intentional torts such as battery are clearly nondischargeable, and it looks to me like John has two strong cases, particularly before me.

HUGHES: It's at a time like this that I'm glad you're a strict constructionist, judge. None of these debts are exempt from discharge if Doe completes his plan, if he pays his taxes and the value of the boat and the car in the next three years or so.

KLINE: You're taking leave of your mind. I may be a strict constructionist and I may pride myself on following the law laid down by Congress, but there's no way Congress could have intended to let you come in here two years after a previous bankruptcy, offer the creditors zilch, and then be given a certificate saying the dischargeability laws don't apply to you. You've got to be kidding!

HUGHES: Judge, with all due respect—you know I have to come before you for fees in this case—Congress said in unmistakable language that the dischargeability laws do not apply, except for support. Sec. 1328(a) says that the discharge given after completion of the plan discharges all unsecured debts except child and spousal support.

BLINN: I guess he's right. Sec. 523(a) expressly applies only to Sec. 1328(b), instances in which the plan is not completed.

GANDY: This is almost too much to swallow. If Hughes is correct, a debtor can get all of the advantages of straight bankruptcy and damn few of the disadvantages by filing Chapter 13. This means that if one of the bank's tellers walks off with $50,000, that obligation is dischargeable in Chapter 13 and not in Chapter 7. Why, come to think of it, I don't see any advantage of straight bankruptcy over Chapter 13.

BLINN: Bob, can you think of anything a debtor can accomplish under Chapter 7 that he cannot under Chapter 13?

HUGHES: No.

KLINE: We may not see very many voluntary Chapter 7s.

This scenario presents an exaggerated example of what could happen if an unconscionable debtor and his attorney chose to employ the provisions of Chapter 13 to the fullest. Obviously, were this to happen on a large scale it would create chaos in such areas as automobile financing. Further, many judges might well choose to define "good faith" in their own terms to forestall confirmation of a plan such as this. Consequently, any debtor or any attorney who considers filing a plan so unfair to creditors should think twice before doing so.

11

Out of debt through Chapter 13: Some typical cases

Debtors who find relief by filing plans under Chapter 13 usually have two things in common: 1) they're in deep financial trouble and are usually distraught about it; 2) they have something to lose—a house, a car, a job, or even a marriage. Otherwise they are of all ages, occupations, and income brackets, for no one group in our society has a monopoly on credit problems. Only one group is rarely found in bankruptcy court—the very poor who have the problems but have nothing to lose.

Let's look at some typical examples of individuals and families who have resolved their financial problems by filing repayment plans under Chapter 13:

John Jones is employed at a steel mill, and his take-home pay is $1,000 a month. He and his wife, Sally, have

four children, the oldest being 13. Life has never been easy
for them, but they've managed fairly well. They live comfortably, the kids are neatly dressed, they support the
church that they attend, and they manage to give the
children a little spending money. Their entertainment
expenses are limited to a movie with the kids once or twice
a month, and a weekly pilgrimage to McDonald's.

John's income has never been sufficient to allow them to
accumulate money for major purchases, or to put anything in the bank, so the Jones's live on credit. They are in
debt for their car, the dental bill for Mary's braces, a
refrigerator and some furniture, and a Household Finance
Corporation loan. They don't quite understand how the
total got that high, but their outstanding obligations are
about $4,000 and the payments nearly $400 a month—and
they never seem to catch up. Every time they near the end
of the payments on one of their debts, some emergency
comes along and they add a new one that is just as large.

Nevertheless, they have managed to get by for years,
with John's paycheck barely adequate to cover their living
expenses and monthly obligations. But not so any more.
For several months they have observed that there is never
enough money left from John's check to pay all the bills.
It is nothing you can put your finger on. They haven't
changed their life-style; in fact, they've tightened their
belts a bit. They are simply the victims of an inflationary
spiral that has driven up the cost of everything they have
to buy.

Like many other debtors, John and Sally found that
every month they fell further and further behind. They
began getting warning notices, dunning letters, and un-
pleasant phone calls from creditors who were displeased
with their failure to pay. Finally, at a friend's suggestion,
they visited a lawyer who recommended that they file
under Chapter 13. The lawyer reviewed their expenses and
pointed out that their living expenses and monthly obliga-

tions totaled $1,200 a month. There was no way they could ever get by, much less catch up, on John's thousand-dollar check.

The lawyer prepared a plan under Chapter 13 under which they agreed to pay their creditors at a reduced rate of $100 a month over a four-year period. This was sufficient to pay their attorney, the administration and trustee's fees, and leave them—after meeting their basic living expenses—with surplus income of $100 a month. Not only will they get out of debt, but for the first time in their lives they will have surplus income that will enable them to plan for the future by opening a savings account.

Bill Bingham, at 39, was a psychological counselor at a local university and part-time staff worker at a state mental hospital. Although his yearly earnings were $20,000, he was overburdened with debt, part of it acquired while he was earning his undergraduate and master's degrees.

Bill wanted a doctorate in clinical psychology, but to earn it he would have to take a two-year leave of absence from his jobs and survive on a grant of $5,000 a year.

Through the flexibility of Chapter 13, Bill was able to complete his studies and obtain his doctorate without creditor harassment and fear of repossession of his furniture and automobile. Small payments were made for two years and then increased after Bill resumed full-time employment.

Bill is now a full professor at a university and on the staff of a local hospital and clinic. He has a gross income of $45,000 a year, is out of debt, married, has a sizeable bank account and investments in the stock market, and is eternally grateful to the friend who told him about Chapter 13.

Ed Livingston, 42 years of age, is office manager for a

wholesale trucking firm; he has two children, was divorced after 15 years of marriage. The divorce decree provided that Ed would pay all of the outstanding credit obligations, alimony, and child support. Ed could not fulfill his financial commitments when there was only one household to support, and with the added expense of his own rent and food, he faced contempt proceedings in the divorce court and creditor harassment on the job.

Ed's impossible situation was resolved through Chapter 13, which reduced his monthly installment credit payments by 65 percent, making it possible, at least, for him to comply with the alimony and child-support order and still have enough for his own basic living expenses.

Today, thanks to Chapter 13, Ed still has his job, has paid off his bills, remarried, and even purchased a home.

Charlie Wilson, 32, with a wife and two children, had a streak of bad luck. Although his job as a traffic manager for a large trucking company was considered a well-paid one, his wife's compulsive spending forced Charlie to file a personal bankruptcy three years ago. Mrs. Wilson's psychological problem continued to worsen, until she finally had to be hospitalized and eventually placed in a private sanitarium.

Charlie had to borrow heavily to cover the medical expenses. His company provided hospitalization insurance, but unfortunately it did not include coverage for psychological disorders. Mrs. Wilson eventually returned home, but the outstanding obligations caused by her illness were overwhelming, with almost one-third of each loan payment being applied against interest.

Through Chapter 13, Charlie was able to pay his creditors in full, saved hundreds of dollars by eliminating all interest and service charges, and reduced his scheduled monthly payment to creditors by over 50 percent.

Tommy Hopkins, age 39, is married and has three children; he is a steel worker. Although Tommy was on his job for 10 years, a strike and a two-month layoff caused him to fall behind on his mortgage, car note, and furniture payments. Tommy had to hide his car from repossessors, and the furniture company tried several times to pick up their furniture. After returning to work, Tommy tried to resume the mortgage payments, but the payments were returned with the notation that all of the arrearage had to be brought current immediately. The auto finance company and the furniture dealer also demanded that their accounts be brought up to date or their security returned.

Tommy had a considerable equity in his house, auto, and furniture, and did not want to lose them. Without borrowing and without jeopardizing any of his equity in his home, auto, furniture, Tommy paid all of his creditors through Chapter 13. The plan proposed that he forward the full current monthly payment due the mortgage company each month, and the mortgage arrears, together with the balances due on the automobile and furniture, were taken care of through the monthly payment Tommy made to the Chapter 13 trustee.

Chapter 13 gave Tommy the breather he needed to get back on his feet, saved his home from foreclosure, and stopped repossession of his automobile and furniture.

Gail Lutz, 29 years old, has three children; she is employed by a bank in a clerical capacity. Gail's husband never seemed able to hold a job for very long, and during each of his periods of unemployment they got further in debt. Finally, when the pressure from creditors reached a peak, and the finance company threatened to repossess their car, Gail's husband solved his problem by disappearing, along with the car. Gail was left with the children and a mountain of unpaid bills.

Through Chapter 13, Gail was able to find an honorable, dignified, and workable solution to her financial problems. Under the protection of the federal court, Gail filed under Chapter 13, automatically staying all further creditor action against her. Gail was able to pay her creditors at a realistic rate over an extended period, while retaining sufficient funds to provide a decent standard of living for herself and the three children. She has few regrets about her husband, but she does miss the car.

Elmer Bruckman, 42 years old, is married and has three children. Elmer, a mechanical engineer, established a corporation to manufacture gears. He soon found that, although he knew a lot about engineering, he didn't know much about running a business. The enterprise folded when he was forced to shut down because he couldn't meet his payroll.

All of Elmer's business assets were liquidated and the proceeds distributed to creditors. Despite the fact that Elmer operated as a corporation, many of the business creditors continued to harass Elmer for payment, and some even filed suit to try to recover the balances due them. Elmer, meanwhile, could hardly cover his personal obligations, much less the outstanding debts owed by the gear company.

After finding employment, Elmer found a way out of debt through Chapter 13. Creditors, including Elmer's business creditors, were enjoined from further dunning or proceeding with their lawsuits. Chapter 13 enabled Elmer to pay off his personal obligations in full and eliminated any further claims made against him by the gear company creditors. Thanks to Chapter 13, Elmer has been able to build a rewarding career with a large corporation in engineering, the field he knows best.

George Anderson, 52, is a man of modest means, but he lives comfortably, using credit only for essential purchases and never beyond the level his income will support. His financial stability was in sharp contrast to the behavior of his younger brother, John, a compulsive spender who yielded to all of the temptations put before him by credit-granting organizations.

Although George was critical of John's free spending habits, he felt obligated to help his brother when he came to him with a plea that he cosign a note. John's salary had been garnisheed by one creditor, and others were closing in. He needed $7,500 to consolidate all of his debts and pay his creditors so the garnishment would be released. The loan company was willing to provide the money if John could find a responsible person to cosign the note.

George was reluctant to sign, reminding John of the many times that he had urged him to reform his spending habits and make an effort to reduce his debts. John replied that he realized he had been foolish, but that he had learned his lesson, and if George would help him out of this one last jam he would tear up his credit cards and never buy anything on credit again.

George cosigned the note and that was the last he saw of his brother for several months. Then he was served a notice that John was delinquent in his payments on the note; demand was made on him to pay the balance owing, in full and at once.

John was distraught. More than $6,000 was still owing on the note. There was no way he could come up with that sum unless he borrowed it, and if he did, the additional monthly payment would throw his own budget out of whack. He called a friend, an attorney who lived in his neighborhood, and told him what had happened. The lawyer told him that the loan company could, indeed, enforce its claim against him, but that there was another way out. If his brother filed a repayment plan under Chapter 13, and agreed to pay the balance over an extended period of time, both he and George would be protected from further action by the creditor.

George was able to persuade his brother to do so and thus escaped any further action by the loan company. He will never cosign another note.

Bruce and Betty, like many other young couples in these inflationary days, overextended themselves to buy a house. They knew that it was unwise to commit more than a quarter of their income to housing payments, but they were fed up with apartment living, and if they abided by that limitation there was no way they could buy a house. When Betty spotted her dream home, she persuaded Bruce that even though the price was beyond the margin of safety, they both were working and could expect to get raises soon that would bring the mortgage payment more in line with what they earned.

The couple bought the dream house, but soon after they moved in, Betty became dissatisfied with the way their old furniture looked in the house. Bruce yielded to her insistence, and they bought several thousand dollars worth of new furniture with no money down. The refrigerator conked out shortly thereafter, so they replaced that. Then Betty became concerned that their old car really didn't look appropriate in the driveway of such a nice new house, so Bruce replaced it, too, reeling a bit with the shock when he found out how much new car prices had risen.

It was not long before the couple had cause to regret the extent to which they had overextended themselves. Everything seemed to cost more than they had planned. They had expected that Bruce's transportation expenses would go up when they moved from a city apartment to a suburban home, but they hadn't anticipated the extent to which gasoline prices would rise. They were getting farther and farther behind on all their payments, and finally began to let the mortgage payment slide, as well.

The day finally arrived when the savings and loan notified them that unless they paid the arrears on their mortgage payment, their property would be foreclosed. Bruce, desperate, went to his lawyer for advice. The attorney suggested that he file a debt repayment plan under Chapter 13. If he agreed to make the regular mortgage payment each month, and catch up the arrears as part of the plan, the court would forestall foreclosure action by the savings and loan.

Bruce took his advice, and today he and Betty will tell you that the best chapter in their lives was Chapter 13!

Tillie and Lou were both employed, Tillie as a secretary clearing $700 a month, and Lou as an account executive for a national advertising agency earned $1,800 a month. When Lou was transferred from New York to the Chicago office, they decided to abandon apartment living. They rented an expensive home in one of Chicago's fashionable suburbs, with the intention of buying in the same community if they liked it there.

Both Lou and Tillie liked nice things, and bought them often, always on credit. They dined out frequently, caught most of the new plays and concerts, and vacationed at the most expensive resorts. Between their life-style and their installment obligations, they lived to the absolute limits of their combined income.

But then the economy began to falter, business began to retrench, and one of the first places to feel it was the advertising budget. This forced the advertising agency to retrench, too, and with 72 hours notice, Lou lost his job.

Lou's first reaction was a confident one. There was always a lot of movement in the advertising business and he knew it wouldn't be long before he found another, perhaps more lucrative, job. After four months of interviews and turndowns he realized that he was deluding himself. In desperation, he accepted a job as a clerk in a department store, at less than half the salary he had formerly earned.

Meanwhile, the couple had been unable to maintain their payments on the car and their furniture, and repossession was threatened unless the accounts were brought to current status at once. Lou knew that, at his reduced salary, they would have trouble meeting the current payments, and had no hope of catching up the arrears.

Through a friend, Lou discovered the existence of Chapter 13. Within 24 hours after consulting a lawyer, he and Tillie filed a composition plan. They proposed, over a three-year period, to pay the actual value of the furniture and the car. In addition, they proposed to pay 10 percent of the remaining unsecured portion of the balance on the furniture and the car, and 10 percent of the balances on their other unsecured accounts.

After the plan had been confirmed, their monthly payments to the Chapter 13 trustee were only half what they had been before. The payment was well within the amount that Lou's reduced income would enable them to pay, and they could kiss all their debts good-bye in three short years.

12

Chapter 13 and
the small businessman

Jim Dodd's wife, Margaret, worked while he attended dental school. Despite the fact that she took time off to have two babies, the couple managed to save $10,000 to help him get started in practice when he got his degree. When Jim graduated they found a pleasant Midwestern town that needed another dentist and Jim decided to establish his practice there.

Jim needed equipment and fixtures for his office, and the sales representative for a dental equipment company referred him to a finance company that specialized in business loans. The finance company agreed to lend Jim the difference between his savings and the cost of the equipment, taking the equipment as collateral for the loan. Eager to get started in his practice, Jim signed the papers despite his shock at learning that he would be paying almost 30 percent interest. He had not realized that some state usury laws do not apply to business loans.

The first couple of years, while Jim was building his practice, were tough sledding. Nevertheless, he was able to support his family comfortably, and meet the monthly payments on his 10-year business loan. After a few months he and Margaret began to acquire some credit cards, and she opened charge accounts at the local department stores. The kids always seemed to be needing something, and the couple reasoned that they must dress well and drive a good car in order to maintain his image as a successful professional man.

Within a couple of years after Jim began his practice the couple had gone into debt to the tune of $146,000, broken down as follows: mortgage balance on their house, $75,000; home improvement loan to finish off a rec room in the basement, $10,000; balance due on business equipment loan, $30,000; balance on automobile, $5,000; various dental suppliers, $10,000; furniture store, $7,000; VISA, $2,500; Mastercharge, $1,500; American Express, $3,000; miscellaneous oil and gasoline charges, $1,000; miscellaneous department stores, $1,000.

Happily, Jim's practice improved steadily, so they were able, with some difficulty, to manage the debt. Then Jim had a heart attack and was unable to work for six months. Although most of Jim's patients were sympathetic and returned when he was again able to work, some found new dentists in the interim and their business was gone.

During his illness the couple at first managed to survive on his accounts receivable, but these ran out before he was able to resume his practice. They fell behind on all of their financial obligations. Even after Jim returned to work, their situation did not improve immediately because it would be a couple of months before cash started coming in from current receivables.

When his practice was at a normal level, Jim had an

income of slightly over $4,000 a month. His living costs and business expenses totaled over $3,500 a month. The difference was far short of the amount required to fulfill their creditor obligations.

With his creditors closing in, Jim called the U.S. trustee at the federal courthouse and got the names of a few attorneys specializing in small business reorganization. After selecting one of them, he was surprised to learn that under the bankruptcy reform act he was now eligible to file a plan under Chapter 13, since he had secured debts of less than $350,000 and unsecured debts of less than $100,000. Jim did not want to file bankruptcy unless there was no alternative, so he was delighted when his attorney advised him that because of the new federal exemptions, and his eligibility for Chapter 13, he would not have to sacrifice any of his material assets, and could even escape with his pride.

The attorney suggested that Jim file a plan to pay 10 percent of the unsecured debts and 100 percent of the value of the secured obligations. The attorney then consulted with an appraiser and determined that the value of the dental equipment was only $13,000, despite the loan balance of $30,000, and that the furniture was worth only $3,500 despite a loan balance of $7,000. The plan would pay the value of the equipment and furniture in full, and 10 percent of the remaining unsecured portion of the obligation. This proved to be $2,050, rather than $20,500 if he had paid for the furniture and equipment in full.

The attorney calculated that with these adjustments Jim's obligations would total $24,695, including an estimated $3,245 in attorney's and trustee's fees. He proposed a plan to pay off these balances at $515 per month over 48 months. Jim would maintain his mortgage and car payments outside the plan.

The lawyer assured him that the court would have to confirm the plan because it would return more to the creditors than a straight bankruptcy would, and thus met the test that it was in the best interests of the creditors.

It was Jim and Margaret's good fortune that small business and professional men are now eligible to file under Chapter 13. Their case is an example that will apply to any sole proprietorship, whether a business or a profession, so long as the unsecured debts are less than $100,000 and the secured debts less than $350,000, and the creditors will receive at least as much under the debtor's plan as they would have received in a bankruptcy liquidation.

13

When Chapter 13 fails

Chapter 13 isn't always the answer. Sometimes it doesn't work. The debtor, well-intentioned though he may be, is unable to adhere to a stringent budget. He may experience new misfortunes that make it impossible for him to hold to the provisions of the plan, such as the loss of the income that is necessary to complete it. He may be unable or unwilling to resist the further use of credit during the period of the plan, with the result that he becomes so overwhelmed with new bills that Chapter 13 is no longer feasible. Or he may decide after a few months of spartan existence that he doesn't want to put up with privation for three to five years, and elect to file bankruptcy instead.

Those who are unable to hold to the terms of their plan through no fault of their own will benefit from the provision that permits them to petition for modification of their plan after it has been confirmed. If they have difficulty in meeting the payment schedule they can, with court approval, alter their plan to reduce the amounts paid to creditors, or extend the period in which payments can be made, so long as the total period of the plan does not exceed five years.

If these changes will not result in a feasible plan they also can petition for a hardship discharge. As a last resort they have the right to convert their Chapter 13 case to a Chapter 7 liquidation at any time, provided that they can comply with the other provisions of the bankruptcy act.

Occasionally, a debtor who is committed to a Chapter 13 plan fails to heed the court's warning to refrain from obtaining additional credit during the period of the plan. He contracts for new obligations which will not be discharged on completion of the plan because they were acquired after confirmation by the court, and approval of the trustee was not first obtained.

In some instances, the magnitude of these new obligations is such that the debtor knows he ultimately will be in a new financial mess because of them. If he completes the plan and is discharged, and it was a composition plan in which he paid less than 70 percent of the amount he owed on his unsecured debts, he cannot file bankruptcy for six full years. If he converts his Chapter 13 case to a Chapter 7 liquidation he may still not receive a discharge on the debts acquired after confirmation of the plan. However, he can ask for a dismissal of the Chapter 13 case and after obtaining it, file under Chapter 7—assuming that he is eligible to do so—and discharge all of his debts, both the old and the new.

Chapter 13 is usually best

It is difficult, under the provisions of the new act, to identify situations in which straight bankruptcy is preferable to Chapter 13. There is really only one situation in which it cannot be used, and a few others in which the debtor, for reasons of his own rather than of law, may choose not to use it.

Chapter 13 cannot be used by a debtor if his income is insufficient to provide for the payment, within the period of the plan, of the value of his secured obligations, some percentage of his unsecured obligations, his lawyer, the trustee's and other administrative fees. Significantly, as noted earlier, the group of debtors who can meet this test was expanded considerably by the provision of the new act which permits a plan, with court approval, to be extended over five years.

The discretionary factors which cause some debtors to choose straight bankruptcy rather than Chapter 13 are these:

1. They don't want to pay their bills and feel no moral obligation to do so. In short, they're deadbeats, and don't care who knows it.

2. They have a major creditor whose bill they regard as unjust, and they file bankruptcy as the only means of escape.

3. They are so incensed by creditor harassment and unscrupulous collection tactics that they see bankruptcy as a delicious form of revenge.

4. They are in one of the "classic" categories— compulsive spenders, alcoholics, gamblers—and know that filing Chapter 13 is pointless, because they will not be able to adhere to the plan.

When bankruptcy won't work

Now let's look at the other side of the coin: the situations in which bankruptcy is not a practical answer, but Chapter 13 may be. Bankruptcy is not a realistic solution for:

1. A debtor who has substantial assets, which are more

than enough to cover his obligations, that he wants to keep. Often, this debtor is simply in trouble because of a liquidity problem. He has real estate which he doesn't want to sell because the market isn't right. He owns stocks which he expects will appreciate substantially in the future, but are undervalued now, so he doesn't want to sell. He has personal property—perhaps valuable antiques that have been in his family for generations—that would realize substantial cash if sold, but for sentimental reasons he doesn't want to sell.

A liquidation is obviously a poor choice for someone in this position. Under Chapter 13 he can retain all of his assets, meet his obligations on a reduced payment schedule, and liquidate his stocks or real estate at a more appropriate time.

2. A debtor who has too many obligations secured by purchase money liens on items—furniture, appliances, an automobile, or motor home—in which he has built up a substantial equity that he does not want to surrender. In a liquidation, he would be forced to return the items or pay their value. Under Chapter 13 he can keep the items by agreeing to pay their *value* in monthly payments under the plan.

3. A debtor who has received a discharge in bankruptcy during the previous six years, or has filed a Chapter 13 composition plan which paid less than 70 percent of unsecured obligation during that same period. He is ineligible to file another bankruptcy until six full years have elapsed, but he can file a Chapter 13.

4. A debtor who has a cosigner on some of his obligations whom he wishes to protect. In a straight bankruptcy case, the cosigner's obligations are not effected, and the creditors will proceed against him even though the debtor is discharged. Under Chapter 13 the cosigners are protected.

5. Debtors who misrepresented their financial situation in order to obtain credit, with the result that their debts

will not be discharged. A creditor in these situations can file an application to determine dischargeability, and if he can prove his case to the court the sum owed him will not be discharged. In a Chapter 13 composition plan the debt will be discharged.

6. Debtors who, because of this same misrepresentation, or other forms of personal misconduct, fear that a creditor may file an objection to discharge. This is an action which challenges the right of the debtor to have *any* of his debts discharged, not merely the one owed the challenger.

Frequently, under the old act, creditors who could file an exception to have their own accounts removed from the discharge threatened to file objections instead. They used the threat as leverage to coerce the debtor into reaffirming his entire debt to them. This form of intimidation should be substantially reduced by another provision of the new law. It provides that a debtor cannot reaffirm an obligation, or, if he does reaffirm one it is not enforceable, unless three conditions have been met: 1) the agreement must be made before the discharge is granted; 2) the debtor has 30 days in which to rescind the agreement and that 30 days has passed without any action by the debtor; and 3) there must be a hearing before the judge prior to the entry of the discharge.

This provision acts as a Miranda-like warning with respect to consumer debt. The judge, before a reaffirmation is approved, must review the proposed agreement and determine that it is in the debtor's best interests. He must advise the debtor that there is no legal obligation to enter into the agreement. The court must conclude that the agreement was entered into in good faith and does not impose an undue hardship on the debtor or a dependent of the debtor. He must inform the debtor that the agreement is not one that is required under the bankruptcy act, advise him regarding its legal effects and consequences, and explain what will happen if there is a default.

The court must also determine whether the agreement that the debtor desires to enter into complies with the bankruptcy act, and that the debt is a consumer debt and not one secured by real property. Settlement can be made of a bona fide claim of a possible exception that is filed to the discharge, or reaffirmation can take place and consist of the redeemed value of the exempt property. The debtor would pay the value of the collateral in installments, provided it conforms to the redemption provisions of the bankruptcy act.

Grounds for exception to discharge

Under Chapter 13 there are only two grounds for exceptions to discharge and the others, which do apply to bankruptcy, have no effect. They may be entered for alimony or support due a former spouse or a child of the debtor under a separation agreement, property settlement agreement, or divorce decree. Those filing bankruptcy must also worry about other exceptions, which include:

1. Debts for some taxes and customs duties.
2. Debts incurred through misrepresentation of the debtor's financial condition, or actual fraud.
3. Debts not listed or scheduled by the debtor to give the creditor adequate notice so that he could file a claim.
4. Debts involving fraud or defalcation while acting in a fiduciary capacity, embezzlement, or larceny.
5. Debts resulting from willful and malicious injury by the debtor to another entity or to the property of another entity.
6. Some debts for fines, penalties or forfeitures payable to a governmental unit.

These exceptions to discharge would apply to a specific claim made by the creditor. In addition, a debtor who files bankruptcy must worry about objections to discharge, which may prevent him from being discharged from any of his debts. The following grounds for objection apply in bankruptcy and may be filed by any party in interest, creditors, or the trustee:

1. The debtor is not an individual.

2. The debtor, with intent to hinder, delay, or defraud a creditor or officer of the estate charged with custody of the property under the act has transferred, removed, destroyed, mutilated, or concealed (or permitted same): a) property of the debtor, within a year before the date of filing of the petition; or b) property of the estate, after the date of filing of the petition.

3. The debtor has concealed, destroyed, mutilated, falsified, or failed to keep or preserve any recorded information, including books, documents, records, papers from which the debtor's financial condition or business transactions might be ascertained, unless such act or failure to act was justified under all of the circumstances of the case.

4. The debtor knowingly and fraudulently or in connection with the case: a) made a false oath or account; b) presented or used a false claim; c) gave, offered, received, or attempted to obtain money, property, or advantage or promise of money, property, or advantage for acting or forbearing to act; or d) withheld from an officer of the estate entitled to possession under the act any recorded information, including books, documents, records, papers relating to the debtor's property or financial affairs.

5. The debtor has failed to explain satisfactorily, before determination of denial of discharge under this paragraph, any loss of assets or deficiency of assets to meet the debtor's liabilities.

6. The debtor has refused, in the case, a) to obey any lawful order of the court, other than an order to respond to

the material question or to testify; b) on the ground of privilege against self-incrimination, to respond to a material question approved by the court to testify after the debtor has been granted immunity with respect to the matter concerning which such privilege was invoked; or c) on the ground other than the properly invoked privilege against self-incrimination, to respond to a material question approved by the court or to testify.

7. The debtor has committed any act specified in paragraph two, three, four, five, or six, on or within one year before the date of the filing of the petition, or during the case, in connection with another case concerning an insider.

8. The debtor has been granted a discharge under sections of the bankruptcy act other than Chapter 13 in a case commenced within six years from the date of the filing of the petition.

9. The debtor has been granted a discharge under Chapter 13 in a case commenced within six years before the date of filing of the petition, unless payments under the plan in such case total at least: a) 100 percent of the allowed unsecured claims in such case, or b) (i) 70 percent of such claims, and (ii) the plan was proposed by the debtor in good faith and was the debtor's best effort.

10. The court approves a written waiver of discharge executed by the debtor after the order for release under this chapter.

Any of these exceptions or objections to discharge can thwart the debtor who endeavors to resolve his financial problems through bankruptcy. None of them applies if he files under Chapter 13. Obviously, any debtor who fears that he is vulnerable to an exception because of any one of these conditions would be well-advised to consider Chapter 13. If he files a composition plan, proposing to pay unsecured creditors ten cents on the dollar, he could escape 90 percent of his obligations. Under Chapter 7, if an exception to discharge were granted by the court, he could not escape at all.

This may, in fact, prove to be an unintended result of the Bankruptcy Reform Act of 1978. Chapter 13 may become a bonanza for irresponsible and immoral debtors, and a nightmare for the credit-granting institutions in the United States.

One final word about exceptions. A debtor who is considering bankruptcy should give careful consideration to the possibility that a creditor may file an objection to discharge, or an exception to discharge.

It is standard practice for banks and consumer finance companies to require that loan applicants fill out a form which asks them to list all of their outstanding debts. Usually, in signing the application, they attest to the statement that they have supplied a full and complete list of their obligations, and have no other debts.

Typically, the space allowed for this information would be adequate only for an engraver trained to inscribe the Lord's prayer on the head of a pin. The consumer, when he runs out of space, is apt to comment on this fact to the loan company employee who is handling this loan. The employee, who will determine the credit status of the loan applicant by contacting the credit bureau, doesn't much care what he puts on the form. Often, he will simply tell the applicant that what he has already listed is satisfactory.

If, after the loan is granted, the debtor pays as agreed, his failure to list all his debts is of no consequence. However, if he can't pay and resorts to bankruptcy, it becomes another matter. One statement on the form noted that the creditor has relied on the financial statement in granting the loan. When bankruptcy is filed, he protests to the court that the debtor obtained the loan by deception, because he failed to list all of his debts. If he can document this assertion, a discharge of the debt may not be granted by the court.

Rather than actually petitioning the court, however, the creditor is more apt to consult the debtor's attorney, and advise him that, unless his claim is reaffirmed, he will file an exception to discharge based on the false financial report. Given that choice, the lawyer probably will advise his client to reaffirm, if he believes the creditor will win the case.

The opportunity to coerce a debtor in this manner has also given rise to a less scrupulous device. A creditor, even though he has little or no chance of winning, *threatens* to file an exception. The debtor, concerned about the extra legal expense involved in entering a defense, and over the possibility that the creditor might somehow prevail, reluctantly decides to reaffirm.

Misuse of these coercive tactics was so common under the old act that the bankruptcy commission recommended that the false financial statement exception to discharge be eliminated for consumer debts. The commission recognized that in most cases there was no intention on the part of the debtor to deceive; he simply followed the creditor's instructions with little understanding of the potential consequences of his actions.

The Congress, in drafting the new act, rejected the commission's suggestion on the grounds that there are actual instances of consumer fraud from which the creditor should be protected. They let this grounds for exception stand, but added some modifications. They recognized that the threat of litigation over this exception to discharge, and the attending cost, were often enough to induce a debtor to reaffirm all or part of his obligation. To discourage this practice, the act requires that if the creditor initiates an action to determine whether a debt is dischargeable, and the debtor prevails, the creditor must bear the cost of the debtor's attorney's fees, as well as any actual pecuniary damage, such as the loss of a day's work, that the debtor may have sustained. The act does not require the debtor to pay the creditor's attorney's fees if the creditor prevails. This provision should restrain creditors from filing such applications unless their case is sufficiently strong that they believe they will prevail.

Nevertheless, anyone contemplating bankruptcy should reflect on the circumstances surrounding his application for credit. Did he fill out a loan application? Did he list all of his obligations, fully and completely? If not, beware!

14

Some observations about bankruptcy

In 1829 Charles Lamb observed, "It has long been my deliberate judgment that all bankrupts of whatsoever denomination, civil or religious, ought to be hanged."

Not everyone of his era would have rendered so harsh a judgment, but it is indicative of the terrible stigma associated with bankruptcy throughout much of human history. That stigma has been ameliorated somewhat, however, with the passage of 150 years. As has been the case with divorce, premarital sex, and other once-stigmatizing taboos, bankruptcy has become more acceptable simply because it has become less unusual. Corporations go bankrupt every day, but society does not condemn the corporate executives who emerge from the wreckage, their personal fortunes intact. Movie stars, rock musicians, professional athletes, and other public figures, who have squandered the millions they earned, routinely file bankruptcy, yet retain their places in the sun.

Many attorneys, observing that credit establishments have more than $100 billion working, and gross profits of over $18 billion a year, argue that they can well afford the estimated $2 billion in annual losses that they incur. They reassure reluctant clients, who are concerned about the morality of bankruptcy, by quoting a 1973 decision of the U.S. Supreme Court. The bankruptcy act, said the court, "relieves the honest debtor from the weight of the oppressive and often unfair indebtedness and permits him a fresh start, free from obligations and responsibility. It gives the debtor a new lease on life and a clear field for the future, unhampered by the pressure and discouragement of preexisting debt."

Others are less sanguine about the effects of this growing acceptance of bankruptcy as the solution to personal financial problems. *Fortune* magazine lamented:

"The fact that bankruptcy is beginning to have a good name may be bizarre, but it's very much in tune with the times. In an age that holds society responsible for the misfortunes of individuals, the personal bankrupt is no longer a failure, but an innocent victim whom the rest of us have an obligation to help. Some people do go broke through no fault of their own and they deserve help, but if Americans blithely assume that every case of bankruptcy is like that, the nation will find itself—well, bankrupt."

Certainly, the *Fortune* argument is not without merit, for the moral fiber of the nation does appear to be disintegrating when one can pick up the newspaper and read advertisements proclaiming that anyone in the country who does not wish to pay his debts has only to walk to the nearest federal court and declare himself a bankrupt. It is inconceivable that our society will ultimately benefit from the notion that "bankruptcy is as American as apple pie."

Yet, for a growing number of our inflation- and credit-ridden population, a mechanism such as bankruptcy or Chapter 13 is appropriate and necessary if they are to be relieved of their burden and be restored as productive members of the human race. Moreover, paradoxically, it is those who most legitimately choose this route, for want of a better choice, who usually feel most stigmatized by it.

This is apparent to anyone who has the opportunity to observe, from day to day, the emotions displayed in bankruptcy court. For the near poor and the once rich alike, bankruptcy is a terrible experience, just like divorce. Typically, the debtors display humiliation, frustration, confusion, and outright terror. Some bankrupts are hostile, others pitifully defiant—pitiful because their defiance masks the emotions that they really feel. Many, both men and women, break down and cry; and even for those for whom, the results are a blessing, the experience is pure hell.

Out of my experience with thousands of cases, I have developed a simple formula for those in financial trouble: Go bankrupt if you must, but given the choice, try to resolve your problems without going to court, or if you must go to court, opt for Chapter 13.

15

Bankruptcy under the new act

It may be some measure of the change in social attitude toward individuals who are insolvent, and seek the protection of the court under the bankruptcy act, that they are no longer called bankrupts, but simply debtors. However, the distinction will probably offer small comfort to the consumer debtor who, under the new act, can be forced into an involuntary bankruptcy based on the mere allegation that he is generally not paying his bills on time.

Under the old act an individual employed for wages could not be thrown into bankruptcy. Involuntary bankrupties were filed against corporations, or individual proprietors and professional people, by creditors who alleged certain acts of bankruptcy on the part of the debtor. Their motivation was the knowledge or presumption on the part of the creditor that the assets of the debtor's estate, when liquidated, would enable them to recover all or at least part of what was due them. They chose to close down the debtor's failing business before the remaining assets, too, were dissipated.

In the past, a creditor has had a formidable array of weapons he could use against a defaulting debtor. In addition to all of the tactics of harassment, there were court judgments, garnishments, wage assignments, repossessions, and foreclosures. The creditor could proceed against the future income of the debtor, or against the debtor's property. Now if the debtor has substantial assets but is not paying his bills, his creditors can also force him into a bankruptcy liquidation to collect what is due.

Options for the debtor

The debtor who is forced into involuntary bankruptcy must make a choice. If his assets fall largely into categories that are exempt from liquidation under the new act, he may choose to allow the bankruptcy to proceed, salvaging what he can from the wreckage. Upon discharge, he may find that he has retained most or all of his physical assets, and is happily free of debts.

The alternative for the debtor, if he has nonexempt assets that he wishes to protect, is to convert the liquidation case to a Chapter 13. If he can propose a feasible plan to the court, he can do this without the creditor's consent, and all of the benefits of Chapter 13 previously described will apply.

The debtor who is forced into an involuntary bankruptcy, or who elects to file bankruptcy himself, will benefit greatly from the liberalization of exemptions under the new act. Under Chapter 7, all of the debtor's property as of the date of filing, and that which the debtor may inherit within 180 days of filing, is considered property of the estate. The debtor has the choice of claiming the exemptions allowed under the federal statute, or under the state statute in the jurisdiction in which the bankruptcy petition is filed. If it is a joint filing of husband and wife, one spouse can take the federal exemption and the other the exemptions provided by the state, if they desire.

Historically, the determination of property exemptions in bankruptcy has been considered within the province of state law. The purpose of the exemptions was to assure that, even if creditors levied on all of the debtor's nonexempt property, he would still retain his basic necessities of life so that he could begin anew, and not be left destitute and a public charge.

Those who drafted the new bankruptcy act observed that most of the state exemption statutes were designed for a predominantly rural society, and included exemptions that were established before inflation had taken its toll. Some state exemption laws, in fact, had not been revised in this century. Consequently, their purpose was largely defeated because the level of exemptions no longer provided the debtor with the basics for a fresh start.

To overcome this deficiency, the new act adopts the position that there is a federal interest in seeing that a debtor who goes through bankruptcy emerges with sufficient resources to begin anew. Allowable federal exemptions are specified and the debtor can make a choice between these and the state exemptions, depending on which offers the greatest advantage to him. This right to choose will prevail unless the state enacts a statute that specifically disallows the federal exemptions.

Federal exemptions generous

As with Chapter 13, once a Chapter 7 bankruptcy case is filed, the automatic stay is operative, and all of the creditor's rights against the debtor become rights against the estate. Creditors must cease pursuing the debtor and seek satisfaction of their claims from the estate. The debtor surrenders all of his nonexempt assets for sale by the trustee, who then distributes the proceeds among the creditors who have filed claims allowed by the court. Exempt property is retained by the debtor.

The federal exemptions are so generous that in most cases a debtor filing bankruptcy will be able to keep virtually all, if not all, of his assets without making any further payment on his debts. The principal exceptions will be assets against which creditors have purchase money liens which the debtor must satisfy in order to retain the property. However, to retain the property the debtor must pay only the market value of the items in question, not the balance due on the account.

Nonpossessory liens, granted by the debtor on property used as security to obtain a loan unrelated to the purchase of the property, and judicial liens, can be set aside under the new act if they interfere with the debtor's right to claim an exemption. The act allows the debtor to take a $7,500 exemption to cover his equity in his residence or other personal property. The exemption is doubled if a husband and wife file jointly. If the debtor had pledged his furniture as security for a personal loan, and chose to claim the current value of the furniture within his $7,500 exemption, the lien against the property could be set aside and he could keep the furniture.

The debtor may also take a federal exemption not to exceed $1,200 for any one motor vehicle. He can take a federal exemption up to and not to exceed $200 in value in household items, furnishings, wearing apparel, appliances, books, animals, crops, or musical instruments that are held primarily for the personal family or household use of the debtor or a dependent of the debtor.

Note that this is $200 *per item!* A debtor could have a thousand or more items covered in these categories and keep them all, provided no one item exceeded $200 in value. But that's not all. If there are items that exceed $200 in value, the debtor can still claim them as exemptions under his $7,500 allowance, provided he has not used that exemption for other purposes.

The debtor can also take a federal exemption of his aggregate interest in jewelry held primarily for personal use of the debtor or a dependent, not to exceed $500 in value, and an aggregate interest not to exceed $750 in value of implements, professional books, or tools of the trade of the debtor or a dependent. However, in both of these cases the so-called "unfilled bin" principle again applies, and values in these items in excess of those allowed can be claimed as part of the unused $7,500 exemption for personal property.

Theoretically, a debtor with no equity in real estate or personal property who had $7,500 in a cash bank account could claim that as an exemption. Also exempt is the debtor's aggregate interest in life insurance or the cash surrender value of life insurance, provided it doesn't exceed $4,000. This applies to policies insuring the debtor or an individual of whom the debtor is the dependent.

Other items exempt under the federal statute include:

1. Professionally prescribed health aids for the debtor or his dependent;
2. The debtor's right to receive—
    (a) a social security benefit, unemployment compensation, or a local public assistance benefit;
    (b) a veterans' benefit;
    (c) a disability, illness, or unemployment benefit;
    (d) alimony, support, or separate maintenance, to the extent reasonably necessary for the support of the debtor or any dependent of the debtor;
    (e) payments under a stock bonus, pension, profit sharing, annuity, or similar plan or contract on account of illness, disability, death, age, or length of service,

to the extent necessary for the support of the debtor or any dependent of the debtor, unless the plans do not qualify under certain portions of the Internal Revenue code or were in effect proposed or designed for fraudulent intent.

3. The debtor's right to receive, or property that is traceable to—

    (a) an award under a crime victim's reparation law;

    (b) a payment on account of the wrongful death of an individual of whom the debtor was a dependent, to the extent reasonably necessary for the support of the debtor and any dependent of the debtor;

    (c) payment under a life insurance contract that insured the life of an individual of whom the debtor was a dependent on the date of such individual's death, to the extent reasonably necessary for the support of the debtor and any dependent of the debtor;

    (d) a payment, not to exceed $7,500, on account of personal bodily injury, not including pain and suffering or compensation for actual pecuniary loss, of the debtor or an individual of whom the debtor is a dependent; or

    (e) a payment in compensation of loss of future earnings of the debtor or an individual of whom the debtor is or was a dependent, to the extent reasonably necessary for the support of the debtor and any dependent of the debtor.

Other benefits in the new act

We have already covered the benefits to debtors in the new act that involved claims made by secured creditors. These rights to redeem secured property amount to the right of first refusal in a foreclosure sale of the property involved. They are extremely important to the debtor because, while the market value of the property involved is often minimal, the replacement cost could be very high. The debtor is often far ahead if he can retain his property, rather than being forced to replace it.

Some debtors get another break in the new act because of changes in the way the exception to discharge for obtaining credit on the basis of a false financial statement is applied. The new act takes the position that such misconduct is better dealt with by an exception to discharge for the debt incurred with the false financial statement than by total denial of discharge. Thus, while the debtor does not escape the debt obtained with the false statement, he is still discharged from all the other indebtedness claimed in his petition.

The provisions for an exception to discharge based on a false financial statement are also somewhat less stringent under the new act. An exception may be filed if the debtor issued a false financial statement in writing in order to obtain a loan on which the creditor reasonably relied, and did so with intent to deceive. It will not be easy for a creditor to prove that false financial information was provided with intent to deceive, rather than because of carelessness, inadvertence, or some other reason. It will be equally difficult for most credit-granting agencies to establish that they "reasonably relied" on the financial statement in granting the loan, since most of them routinely check with the credit reporting agencies, and their inquiry is a matter of record.

In those cases in which the original loan is made on the basis of a false financial statement, and new money is advanced under a subsequent loan that is not based on a new fraudulent financial statement, only the original amount of the loan can be excepted from discharge. However, if a loan is issued with no fraudulent representations on the part of the debtor, and subsequently rolled over and increased on the basis of a false financial statement, the entire loan can be excepted from discharge.

Claims arising from liability for personal injury

Uninsured motorists involved in automobile accidents resulting in injury to other persons often find themselves saddled with large judgments awarded the victim by sympathetic juries. The payment of judgments ranging in the tens of thousands of dollars is unrealistic for most individuals, so often the only way out of the mess is through bankruptcy. Most claims stemming from injuries sustained in automobile accidents are dischargeable, but there are some technicalities that anyone in this position should bear in mind.

Under the old act, bankruptcy would not discharge an unliquidated claim. If an individual is faced with a potential liability resulting from an automobile accident, one could not file for bankruptcy until after the injured party has filed a lawsuit. If he filed for bankruptcy before the suit is filed, even though he receives a discharge, the aggrieved party is not bound and still can proceed against the bankrupt in a civil action. However, under the new bankruptcy code all contingent or unmatured claims are to be liquidated by the bankruptcy court in order to afford the debtor complete relief.

Second, bankruptcy will not discharge a claim of this nature if the victim is able to establish that the injuries were caused by some willful, intentional, and malicious act of the bankrupt. This is difficult for a victim to prove, and it is almost necessary for a state court to enter a special finding of malice before such a debt becomes nondischargeable. However, it is something to be aware of and to remember before you get so angry at a tailgater that you decide to run him off the road.

The act also covers another problem that has plagued uninsured bankrupts who have had their licenses suspended or revoked because judgments were issued against them that they could not pay. It codifies a decision first reached by the Supreme Court in 1971 in the case of Perez vs. Campbell. In that case Arizona refused to renew a driver's license because the driver had been in an automobile accident, had been sued and lost.

The driver in this case was uninsured, so he filed bankruptcy and was discharged, but Arizona had a general policy that denied a driver's license to any motorist who failed to pay a judgment arising out of an automobile accident. The Supreme Court held that if such a policy were applied to include nonpayment by reason of a discharge in bankruptcy, the policy would run afoul of the federal bankruptcy policy of insuring the debtor a fresh start. The Supreme Court ordered the license issued.

The 1978 bankruptcy act codifies this decision and similar discrimination against bankrupt debtors by governmental agencies, but not by private enterprise. There are many other examples of discrimination against bankrupts. Municipalities have dismissed employees such as firemen or policemen because of bankruptcies. Various state and federal laws automatically deny certain licenses to an individual wholly on the basis of a bankruptcy. These practices are obviously detrimental to a debtor's fresh start and consequently contrary to bankruptcy policy.

The courts have followed the Perez doctrine in some of these other instances, but it is a developing doctrine and more case law will be required before there is a clear outline of the extent of discrimination that is contrary to bankruptcy policy. The new act, however, does establish one principle. It prohibits action by a governmental unit—federal, state, city, or a governmental agency—that is based solely on the filing by a debtor under the bankruptcy code. The prohibition does not extend to examination of the factors surrounding the bankruptcy, the imposition of financial responsibility rules if they are not imposed only on former bankrupts, or on the examination of respective financial condition or managerial ability. The purpose of the section is to prevent an automatic action against an individual for availing himself of the protection of the bankruptcy laws, without denying the right of a licensor or prospective employer to examine and consider the circumstances surrounding a bankruptcy.

Student loans

The indications are that increasing numbers of former college students are going bankrupt to wipe out student loans. Under the former bankruptcy act, educational loans owing to a governmental unit or a nonprofit institution of higher education were not dischargeable unless they first became due more than five years before the filing of the petition, or excepting such a debt from discharge would impose an undue hardship on the debtor or his dependents. Because of a quirk in the new law this exception was inoperable during a period beginning on November 6, 1978, but the exception was reinstated when the remaining provisions of the new act took effect on October 1, 1979.

The procedure to follow in order to obtain a discharge of a student loan is for the debtor to file an application, before the discharge is entered, to determine the dischargeability of the debt. The court can then make a determination as to whether repayment of the loan by the bankrupt would impose an undue hardship on him or his dependents. An example of a case in which a discharge was granted involved a Connecticut woman with a graduate degree in social work. Due to a psychological disorder she was unable to hold down a regular job, but had to support herself and a daughter who was quite ill. The court determined that the best the woman could hope for was to be able to take care of the basic necessities for herself and her daughter. Thus, a clear showing was made of hardship and the educational loan was discharged.

Under the new act a debtor could also escape virtually all of his obligation by filing a composition plan under Chapter 13. The plan could propose payment of as little as one percent of the obligation over a three- to five-year period, and it would be approved if the court found that the plan was proposed in good faith, and that the payment was at least what the creditor would have recovered had the debtor been able to file bankruptcy.

There are those who contend that young people who use bankruptcy to wipe out student loans have simply "found an easy way to get off the hook." Others maintain that the banks that made the loans are shoving young people into bankruptcy so that they can collect the government guarantees on the defaulted loans. My own feeling is that these kids are basically honest, and not intent on ripping off the government. However, they often find themselves, on graduation, unable to find a job, or unable to find one that pays more than what they require for a minimal existence. They simply are not in a position to pay off their student loans.

When the banks begin to apply pressure for repayment of the loans, the former students may literally be forced to file bankruptcy. If the government and the banks were willing to grant these debtors some form of moratorium on repayment until they were able to establish themselves and develop the capacity to repay, there would be fewer bankruptcies. Ultimately, I believe, most of these obligations would be repaid.

Remedies for defects in old act

Most creditors have developed techniques that, in the past, enabled them to avoid the effects of a debtor's bankruptcy and the bankrupts suffered accordingly. Often, the debtors emerged from bankruptcy little better off than they were before. Overbroad security interest in all of a consumer's household and personal goods, reaffirmation of secured debts, limited state exemption laws, and litigation over the dischargeability of certain debts, all contributed to a consumer debtor's post-bankruptcy plight.

In addition, as observed previously, an overly stringent and formalized Chapter 13 wage earner plan discouraged overextended debtors from arranging extended repayment plans. The hearings before the congressional bankruptcy subcommittees indicated strongly that most consumer debtors would rather work out repayment plans, but were compelled to choose straight bankruptcy because the old Chapter 13 did not meet their needs. Only in certain limited areas of the country where bankruptcy judges had taken an active interest, had been willing to put in the extra effort required to make Chapter 13 work, and had encouraged the bar to recommend its use, had Chapter 13 provided any substantial or realistic alternative to straight bankruptcy liquidation.

Meanwhile, in other areas, inadequate supervision of debtors attempting to perform under wage earner plans had made them a way of life for some debtors. Extension of plans, and newly incurred debts, sometimes put debtors under court supervised payment plans for as long as 10 years. This was little more than indentured servitude, for it lasted for an indefinite period without providing the fresh start for the debtor that the bankruptcy act intended.

The bankruptcy system itself, under the old law, also contributed to the ineffectiveness of the bankruptcy remedy. An uncomfortably close relationship between the bankruptcy judge and the trustee often converted a no asset case into a nominal asset case. These were situations in which enough assets were available to pay only the expenses of administration, primarily the trustee's fee and the lawyer's fee, and nothing to the creditors. The old bankruptcy act encouraged this practice by allowing the trustee up to $150 as a fee for his services no matter what the size of the estate, when the assets available were inadequate to compensate the trustee on the usual percentage basis. There were cases of a trustee selling an automobile back to a debtor for $150, or collecting a small income tax refund from a debtor, solely to pay the trustee's own fees.

The new bankruptcy act attempts to cure these inadequacies of the old law and prevent the frequent problems confronting consumer debtors that have occurred both in and out of bankruptcy court. The simplification and expansion of Chapter 13 to include individuals with a regular income is one example. Second, many of the provisions in the old act that enabled private action to undo the beneficial effect of bankruptcy are changed. Third, the debtor is helped by the more generous exemptions and other protections to insure that bankruptcy will provide a fresh start. Finally, the bankruptcy system is modified to eliminate the close relationship between a bankruptcy judge and a trustee that has sometimes worked to the consumer debtor's detriment.

Is new act too generous?

It is now conceivable for a debtor to file a bankruptcy and still retain an automobile, his real estate, all of his furniture, clothing, household possessions, trade tools, jewelry, paintings, and even a camper trailer or a boat. In addition, although he is filing bankruptcy because he is presumably insolvent and unable to pay his bills, the debtor could retain thousands of dollars of cash in a bank account and still have all of his debts discharged. It is not inconceivable that a husband and wife filing jointly could retain assets valued at $30,000 or more and still emerge from bankruptcy court with all of their debts discharged.

Only time and experience with the new act will tell whether the Congress, in attempting to provide greater protection for the honest debtor who is in financial difficulty through no fault of his own, has created a vehicle for legalized fraud. An unprincipled individual without concern for his reputation could employ the generous provisions of the act to deliberately enrich himself at his creditors' expense.

Any individual with an established credit rating, a wallet full of credit cards, and a detailed knowledge of the workings of the new act could devise a plan to amass a small fortune in exempt possessions, travel abroad, and live like a millionaire for months. When his creditors finally caught up with him he could file a bankruptcy petition, pay a $60 filing fee, and win a discharge that allowed him to retain all of his assets and emerge from court debt-free!

16

A bankruptcy case history

Frank Campbell, 38, is married and has two children who are nine and twelve years old. After working for five years as the Midwest representative for several well-known New York manufacturers of women's clothing, Frank decided to open a retail women's apparel shop. He felt that he knew the business well and had the contacts to obtain merchandise and credit.

While employed, Frank had earned at least $50,000 a year, and had purchased a $90,000 home with a down payment of only $10,000. His work had required a great deal of travel, so Frank had acquired all of the major credit cards, including airline and major oil company cards. He drove a late model car, and because he used it for business, his wife Ethel also had a car to enable her to get around their suburban community when he was away.

Frank had saved nearly $10,000, which enabled him to lease a location in a suburban shopping center and stock it with an inventory worth more than $100,000. The shop was leased on November 1, and by December 1 construction had been completed, sales people employed, and the excited couple opened their store for business. Because of Frank's long-time relationships with manufacturers, they had been able to stock the store with the most attractive merchandise, they had a choice location, and they were confident that the shop would enjoy instant success.

Frank and Ethel may have been right about their prospects, but they never had a chance to find out. Early in December the snow began to fall and never seemed to stop. Driving was almost impossible, and even the public transportation facilities broke down. Many people could not get to work, much less do any but the most essential shopping. There were no customers in the new store, and often no employees either.

Although Frank's savings had been enough to get the store ready and stock it well, there was little cash left for working capital. He had counted on rapid cash flow and substantial profits to enable him to pay his rent and his employees, and to maintain a stock of attractive merchandise. But there was no cash flow and, although Frank tried to keep his cool, he soon became frantic. Merchandise had to be moved, so he began having sales and they never stopped. January and February brought weather as severe as that of December, and despite the sales the customers were still few and far between.

Inevitably, creditors began to press Frank for payment—even those whom Frank had once represented. He was using the proceeds from the sales he did make to pay the overhead and the family's living expenses, and the creditors had to wait. His credit was cut off, he couldn't replace the merchandise that was sold, and his inventory was slowly disappearing from the shelves.

By the time the weather improved and customers began buying again, Frank's stocks had dwindled to the point that he could no longer meet his potential customers' needs. Unable to raise additional capital, Frank was compelled to close the store.

Frank's cars were about to be repossessed and one creditor had already obtained a judgment and garnisheed Frank's checking account. In desperation, Frank contacted a job lot buyer in the hope of selling his entire inventory. If he could obtain a decent price, he hoped that the funds realized would enable him to reach an out of court settlement with his creditors. Unfortunately, the merchandise was already out of season and the best offer Frank could get was 30 percent of its value.

Frank went back to work, picking up some of his old lines as a manufacturer's representative. However, some of his old accounts were now disgruntled creditors, so he couldn't get all of them back. He was able to earn only enough to cover his personal living expenses and obligations. There was no way he could pay off over $100,000 in debts incurred in opening the apparel shop.

Creditors were making life miserable for Frank and Ethel, and they decided to seek professional help. The attorney they consulted first suggested the possibility of filing under Chapter 13, but after reviewing Frank's fixed living expenses and his anticipated income, and taking into consideration the personal taxes that would have to be paid, he changed his mind. It was clear that, at least for several months, Frank's income would hardly cover fixed living expenses, plus the arrears on mortgage payments that Frank would have to pay in order to keep his house.

Under the circumstances, bankruptcy appeared to be a realistic solution. Frank and Ethel at first demurred. They held the misconception that a bankruptcy liquidation meant that they would lose their house, their car, their furniture—everything they owned. They were astonished when the attorney told them that this was not the case.

The lawyer explained that under the new federal exemptions in the bankruptcy reform act they could file a joint petition and claim up to a $15,000 exemption for their home, which was actually more equity than they had. The house had been purchased recently with a $10,000 down payment and had not had a chance to appreciate in value, so they had to use only $10,000 of their $15,000 exemption to preserve their equity.

The attorney said that the remaining $5,000, under the "unfilled bin" principle, could be applied against other personal property. They would be allowed to keep all items of household furnishings, household goods, appliances, wearing apparel, musical instruments, and other personal property, so long as the value of any single item did not exceed $200. Individual items that exceeded that value could be retained by using the remaining $5,000 in the "unfilled bin."

Ethel was concerned about her jewelry, and learned that its value up to $500 was exempt, and any additional value could be covered out of the remaining $5,000 of exemption. This could also be used to cover the $1,500 that Ethel had kept tucked away in a savings account, unbeknownst to Frank, to be used in the event of any last, desperate emergency. The cash surrender value in their insurance policies would also be exempt.

Frank and Ethel were delighted to learn that their lawyer could obtain an order setting aside the $10,000 lien on their house which had been obtained by a judgment creditor. The security agreement on their household furnishings, which Frank had given in order to secure a loan from a small loan company, could also be set aside. In both instances the liens impaired exemptions which the debtors were entitled to under the new bankruptcy act.

The "fresh start" concept underlying the new act could not be more apparent than in Frank and Ethel's case. A trustee was appointed to take over the remaining fixtures in the shop and all of the items were sold at public auction, with the proceeds being distributed to creditors after deduction of administrative expenses. Frank and Ethel lost none of their personal possessions, household goods, automobiles, or insurance policies, and even had the liens on their real estate and household goods set aside.

Ethel's concern that bankruptcy would make it impossible for them to obtain future credit was dispelled within days after their bankruptcy had been discharged. Letters began arriving from credit merchants and automobile dealers advising them that despite the bankruptcy, their credit was still good. And why not? The couple was now debt-free and couldn't file another bankruptcy for six full years.

Frank and Ethel have resisted the temptation. After one traumatic bout with creditor harassment they aren't ready to risk another. But if they change their minds, and get in trouble again, there is still a way out. They can, despite the bankruptcy, always file a Chapter 13.

17

Do-it-yourself bankruptcy

It is quite possible for any debtor to do his own bankruptcy without the services of a lawyer. It is also possible for him to pull his own teeth without a dentist, or for a woman to deliver her own baby without a doctor. Possible, yes, but unless you want to risk the potential agony and complications, it isn't recommended.

In addition to the firms that advertise do-it-yourself bankruptcy kits, there are books which outline the requirements for filing your own bankruptcy, and provide samples of the forms that are required. They are not terribly complicated, and any person of reasonable intelligence can probably fill them out. The problem, however, is not with filing the case. It is with all of the complications that may arise before the discharge is entered. The attorney's fees are a small price to pay to insure that your petition yields the discharge that you expect.

Actions that are relatively simple for a bankruptcy lawyer may be terribly complex for a debtor who doesn't know
his way around the law or the bankruptcy court. Even
though he files bankruptcy, the debtor still must deal with
many creditors, and particularly those who are secured. He
must determine whether he wishes to return the security or
keep it, and if he wishes to keep it, he must work out terms
acceptable under the bankruptcy act. Other creditors may
file applications to determine dischargeability, or objections to discharge, and may prevail unless they are confronted by an attorney who knows the law.

Although the filing of a bankruptcy automatically stops
all further garnishments, a petition for a turnover order
may become necessary to release wages held under previous garnishments. A court order for this purpose is not
always easily obtained.

Despite the protection of the automatic stay of further
collection efforts on the part of creditors, harassment of
the debtor does not always stop overnight. Most large
firms have computerized collection systems which do not
respond immediately to an order of the court. Despite the
fact that a debtor files a bankruptcy petition and notice of
the stay order is given, it may be months before the computer is reprogrammed and the notices stop coming.

Bankruptcy judges, pressed by a volume of cases, do not
take the initiative and warn creditors, or haphazardly
throw them in jail, when advised by a debtor that the
creditors are still making threats. A formal petition for a
rule to show cause why the particular creditor should not
be held in contempt must be filed, and a hearing held,
before the bankruptcy judge will issue any order.

Bankruptcy is a very serious matter which should not be
taken lightly and the debtor, for his own protection,
should have a lawyer looking over his shoulder. The
debtor has an obligation to list all of his debts, whether he
intends to pay them or not. He must also declare all of his

assets. Failure to do so may result in an objection to discharge being filed by one of the creditors, but that's not all. There may be criminal sanctions stemming from the falsification of schedules listing obligations or assets. Indictments based on bankruptcy frauds are not common but certainly should be viewed as a threat by debtors involved in financial manipulations that have gone sour.

The debtor may be playing a dangerous game if he tries to save some money by using cut-rate lawyers through legal clinics, or a do-it-yourself bankruptcy kit. Dollars saved are certainly little consolation if the bankrupt finds that his bankruptcy is denied and he is also under a federal criminal indictment.

Most conscientious bankruptcy lawyers will acknowledge that bankruptcy is necessary for only a small fraction of those they see who have financial problems. More often than not they solve their client's problems by using other alternatives. The "do-it-yourself" advertisements, which indiscriminately advise debtors to file bankruptcy as a matter of right, and assert that "you have nothing to lose but your debts," are both inappropriate and false. Bankruptcy is not the answer for everyone, and even those who will benefit from it may not get the full protection of the law if they fail to obtain legal advice.

I've tried to cover the salient features of the bankruptcy act in this book, but there are scores of quirks and technicalities, some based on case history under the act, that could not possibly be covered. The bankruptcy laws are quite complex, and the debtor needs a lawyer who is proficient in both federal and state law. Exemptions allowed bankrupts are not automatic, and property that could be exempted is often lost by debtors who fail to claim it properly.

Generally, the victims of poor advice concerning bankruptcy are the poor, the uneducated, the unsophisticated individuals who should never have filed bankruptcy in the first place, the do-it-yourself bankrupts who have no lawyer, the bargain-hunting client who looks for the cut-rate lawyer in the newspapers, legal aid clinics, or prepaid service plans. They often wind up worse off after filing bankruptcy than they were before. Many of these ill-advised bankrupts have lost their cars, their homes, and other assets that they could have kept if they had engaged competent counsel before embarking on the sometimes irreversible voyage through the bankruptcy court.

One of the most common fates of the "do-it-yourselfers" is to appear in court and discover that a number of creditors have lien rights on their property, all of which the debtors thought was exempt. The bankruptcy act, as explained before, offers a way out of this dilemma for many creditors, but the procedure is a technical one, and it is not the job of the bankruptcy judge or the trustee to act as lawyer for the debtor.

Paint your own house or fix your own plumbing, if you will, but if you want the best shake in bankruptcy court, don't try to be your own lawyer. Be wary, too, of the lawyer you choose, until he has demonstrated that he intends to explore all the alternatives, and will recommend bankruptcy only as a last resort. A competent and ethical attorney will seek the solution that is best for his client, not the one that is simplest and most lucrative for him.

18

This drama doesn't deserve an encore

Logic would dictate that anyone who has been stung would stay away from beehives, but the needs and pressures of our credit-oriented society are such that most bankrupts are eager to reestablish their credit once again. Often, this compulsion is not prompted by a desire to use the credit, but rather by the feeling that if they can obtain it, any stigma resulting from the bankruptcy will be erased.

Obtaining credit after bankruptcy has not, in my experience, been a difficult problem for most of those who have filed under Chapter 13, or taken straight bankruptcy. In fact, it is easier to obtain credit than it is to learn to use it wisely. Some institutions will refuse credit to bankrupts, but if a consumer is persistent he ultimately will find credit grantors ready, willing, and able to finance his purchases. If payments are made promptly to those who do grant credit, the debtor ultimately will rebuild his credit record to the point that he can even secure credit from those who were victims in the bankruptcy that he filed.

Once you file for bankruptcy your creditors know that you cannot file again for six full years, and because your bankruptcy probably wiped out most of your debts you are probably a better credit risk than you were before. Consequently, many businesses actually comb the court lists of bankruptcy filings, and actively solicit those who have filed. As one of my clients told me, "I'm not going to get caught by the vultures again. I had to shut myself up in a room with no phone. I had to fight myself to beat off the temptations."

While credit is important, and almost essential to those in occupations that require extensive travel and entertainment, it certainly is in the best interests of one who has gone through bankruptcy to stay away from it for a while, and try to live on a cash basis. This is especially true of those who find temptation hard to resist. The wise bankrupt is one who profits from his experience and spends only what he must until he has built up a cash reserve that will tide him over if he experiences any financial emergencies in the future.

Realistically, it would be to the debtor's benefit if creditors would not grant credit as readily as they do. Even most attorneys who specialize in bankruptcy and Chapter 13 are not equipped to offer financial counseling services to debtors. Consequently, although the debtor resolves his immediate financial problems, he does not always learn to correct the behavior that got him in financial trouble in the first place. He is not prepared to take the steps necessary to avoid the same pitfalls in the future. Hopefully, as consumer credit problems become more widespread, attorneys will adopt a more meaningful approach and incorporate financial counseling into their practice.

Examples of post-bankruptcy problems

Consider the situation of a client of mine—a young man I'll call Pete. He spent his childhood in extreme poverty with a family whose main concern was getting enough to eat. He failed to complete high school and because of limited skills and education was qualified only for the most menial jobs.

Even though his income was limited, Pete's lifetime of deprivation made him easy prey for the installment merchants, and he became another victim of our buy-now/pay-later society. He found that with small down payments he could acquire many luxuries that had so long been denied him. Within a year he found himself hopelessly in debt. Although he hopped from one menial job to another in an effort to escape them, his wages were repeatedly garnisheed by his creditors.

Pete finally came to me and it almost immediately became clear that his only solution was bankruptcy. We were quite concerned about Pete's ability to stay away from credit once he received his discharge, but Pete assured me that once he was free of his debts he would operate on a strictly cash basis. The day Pete went to court for the first meeting of creditors he appeared enormously relieved to be rid of the pressure, and looked forward to escaping the terrible burden of debt that he'd been carrying.

When we parted company after the court hearing he assured me that he had indeed learned his lesson, and thanked me profusely for the services my office had rendered. I was pleased by his apparent sincerity and determination, but the pleasure was of short duration. I hadn't been back in my office for five minutes before I got a telephone call from one of the local credit jewelers. Pete had left the bankruptcy court and gone directly to the jewelry store, where he attempted to purchase a $1,000 diamond ring. The jeweler was checking to make certain that Pete had filed bankruptcy because if he had, he would be out of debt, able to pay for the ring, and ineligible to file bankruptcy again until six full years had passed.

Some people will not stop buying on credit despite the traumatic experiences that they have gone through. In more than 20 years of bankruptcy practice, I have developed a list of clients who show up like clockwork to file bankruptcy once every six years.

If you apply the classic values to this behavior, these debtors are deserving of little sympathy. The reality is that these repeat bankruptcies are usually brought about by a lack of education, job skills, and social orientation that prevents certain debtors from earning enough to maintain a reasonable standard of living. They are barely able to eke out an existence, never have any surplus cash to put aside for emergencies, and can acquire the desired possessions that most of their friends enjoy only by using credit or borrowing money that they will never be able to repay. Their problem will be solved only when they are provided with educational programs that will provide them with job skills and counseling in financial management.

Another typical case

Consider also the case of Sarah, a woman whose husband left her with five children to support. She managed to find employment which enabled her to provide the basic living expenses for her family, but was unable to keep up with the installment obligations that had been incurred before her husband left. She tried hard, but her best was not good enough; before long her employer advised her that there was a wage assignment that would have to be honored unless Sarah was able to obtain a release.

Sarah was fearful that the wage assignment might cause her to lose her job, so she called the creditor in an effort to obtain a release. She explained that her husband had left her, and that with five children to support she was having a difficult time. Would the creditor, she asked, accept modest installment payments until the obligation was retired, and meanwhile release the wage assignment?

The unrelenting creditor refused to accept the installment program, but offered to release the wage assignment upon receipt of $100. Sarah told him that she didn't have the money and couldn't pay it, but the creditor would not budge. In desperation, Sarah visited several local loan companies, but the story was always the same. After obtaining a list of Sarah's debts and checking with the credit bureau, the loan managers invariably refused the loan. Sarah was obviously a prime candidate for bankruptcy, and they were not about to advance money to her that they could not recover if she went that route.

When Sarah discovered that, despite her good intentions, there was no source from which she could obtain funds to release the wage assignment, she found her way to my office. After reviewing her situation it was clear that bankruptcy was the only solution, so a petition in her behalf was filed. Within days Sarah received telephone calls from two of the loan companies that had refused her previous request, telling her that she could come in and pick up the money for which she had applied.

By checking court records, the loan managers had learned that Sarah's bankruptcy had been filed. With her debts out of the way, and six years in which they could collect on a new obligation, the loan companies now regarded Sarah as a good risk. To Sarah's credit, she refused.

The most unfortunate aspect of this situation is the fact that merchants who prey on bankrupts are usually those whose product is inferior and prices unconscionably out of line. They know that most bankrupts are concerned about their ability to obtain credit and rebuild their credit rating, and will often leap at the opportunity to do so. A lot of expensive junk merchandise is sold every day to consumers who, on the surface, would appear to be the worst possible credit risks.

19

Questions
most debtors ask

The information presented in this book can best be summarized by answering the questions most frequently asked by financially troubled debtors during more than two decades of experience in dealing with consumer financial problems:

What is bankruptcy?

Bankruptcy is a federal legal process that is designed to provide a fresh start for those who are unable to meet their financial obligations. The debtor who files a bankruptcy petition offers to turn over to a trustee appointed by the court all of his assets that are not covered by specific exemptions. The trustee then sells the assets and, after payment of administrative expenses, distributes the bal-

ance of the funds realized to the various creditors. The
debtor is then discharged from his debts, and can begin life
anew, unencumbered by the weight of financial obligations that were beyond his ability to pay.

Are poor people the only ones who file bankruptcy?

No, in fact, the very poor are the least likely to file
because they have nothing to lose, and thus little to fear
from their creditors. The bankruptcy court is visited by a
broad cross section of the population, most of whom are
in the middle- or upper-income brackets. The bankruptcy
judges are accustomed to seeing movie stars and entertain-
ers who have earned millions, doctors, lawyers, carpenters,
in addition to plumbers, assembly line workers, white
collar workers, and Americans in every other conceivable
occupation. They have one thing in common: they owe
more than they are able to pay.

Is there more than one kind of bankruptcy?

Yes, the bankruptcy act includes different provisions for
corporations, municipalities, commodity brokers, and consumers. Consumers, under the act, have two options. They
can file a straight bankruptcy under Chapter 7, in which
their nonexempt assets are liquidated to pay their creditors, or they can file under Chapter 13. This chapter
provides an opportunity for persons with a regular income
to present a plan for repayment of all or part of what they
owe, without giving up their assets. Upon successful completion of the plan, their debts are discharged.

How often can you file bankruptcy?

After filing a bankruptcy you cannot file another for six
full years. However, if you experience new financial difficulties you can file a plan under Chapter 13.

How will bankruptcy effect my credit rating?

After what you've been through, you shouldn't ask. Why risk getting in trouble again? However, your bankruptcy will remain on the records of the credit bureau for 14 years and may or may not effect your ability to obtain credit in the future. Some credit-granting organizations refuse to extend credit to bankrupts as a matter of policy, at least until some time has passed and they have succeeded, through prompt payment of their obligations, in demonstrating that they have learned how to manage their affairs. Other creditors welcome the opportunity to do business with bankrupts. They reason that the bankrupt has improved his ability to pay by eliminating all of his debts, and because he must wait six years to file another bankruptcy, they have that period in which to collect.

One of my friends cosigned a note with me. If I go bankrupt will he still be responsible for that debt?

If you failed to make payments your creditor could seek payment from your cosigner without even attempting collection from you. The new Chapter 13 provides an automatic stay of collection attempts against a cosigner, and if you receive a discharge of your debts after completing your plan, your cosigner's obligation is discharged, too, provided the obligation was paid in full.

Do I have to list all of my debts when I file bankruptcy?

Yes, the law requires that you list all of your obligations, whether you intend to pay them or not. However, the scheduling of an obligation does not prevent you from paying the creditor voluntarily at a later date.

Is there some minimum amount I must owe in order to file bankruptcy?

No, but it makes no sense to consider filing unless you owe a substantial amount. Bankruptcy is a valuable right, and it would be foolhardy to file for a minimal amount and thus lose the right to file again for six full years. You may need the protection more desperately later on.

Can't I stop a creditor from suing me by making a partial payment of what I owe?

No, this is a popular fallacy, but it isn't true. You may forestall collection action by making partial payments, because it is evidence that you do want to pay, but doing so doesn't legally restrain the creditor from filing a lawsuit against you. In most cases, you have made a promise to pay a specific amount at specific times. Failure to fulfill the commitments made in this installment program, even though you make partial payment, will put the creditor in a position to file suit. If he sues, he will probably demand payment of the entire unpaid balance of the installment plan.

How does a person decide whether or not to file bankruptcy?

The best way to make the decision is to consult a competent attorney who is qualified in the bankruptcy area. A full financial disclosure must be made to the lawyer to enable him to make a proper evaluation of the debtor's financial situation. Consideration must be given to all of the advantages and disadvantages of bankruptcy filing after exploring all of the possible alternatives. It is vital that the attorney have all the facts, and you need not fear giving them to him because the relationship between an attorney and a client is completely confidential.

What alternative to bankruptcy is there for a debtor who

can't pay, and whose creditors won't accept reduced pay-ments?

Sometimes creditors who refused to accept a reduced payment plan proposed by a debtor will accept it when it is offered by an attorney. This is because they realize that if they refuse, the debtor's next move will probably be to bankruptcy court. If they refuse to accept a voluntary plan, the debtor should consider filing under Chapter 13. This is a section of the bankruptcy act that enables persons with a regular income to repay their creditors on a reduced pay-ment schedule spread over three to five years. Such plans can be confirmed by the court even though the debtor proposes to pay only a percentage of his total obligations, and when he completes the plan all of his debts are dis-charged.

Does filing either a Chapter 13 or a bankruptcy cause the debtor to lose his job?

It isn't likely, although if a bank president were to file, it might cause him some problems. Actually, most employ-ers aren't even notified when a debtor files under either Chapter 7 or Chapter 13 of the bankruptcy act. Even if they are notified, the odds are that they will be delighted that the employee has taken an affirmative step to resolve his financial problems. The employer realizes that with the financial pressures removed, the employee should be more productive and better able to concentrate on his job.

Should a spouse always join in filing a bankruptcy?

There is a diversity of opinion among bankruptcy law-yers as to whether the spouse should file, especially if the spouse has not signed for most of the obligations owed. I have always felt that, even if the spouse is not employed, it

is best to provide her with peace of mind and protection
from a potential hassle with bill collectors, by filing a
joint petition. This would also avoid a problem at some
future time should the spouse return to work, or attempt
to purchase real estate while creditors were taking action
to perfect liens against her.

Some states have family expense statutes making the
spouse who has not signed for an obligation responsible
for purchases made by the other spouse, provided that the
purchases were enjoyed by the family. In family expense
states, this spouse would have to raise a defense in the state
court and obtain a determination from the judge as to
whether the items purchased actually are family expense
items. This would have been avoided had both spouses
filed for bankruptcy.

*My wife and I are in the process of getting a divorce and
I'm simply not going to be able to pay alimony and child
support, my own separate maintenance, and all of the
installment obligations. I'll have to file bankruptcy, but
wonder whether my wife should file, too.*

This can be an extremely perplexing situation. The
primary obligation of the working spouse is to provide for
the support and maintenance of the former spouse and
children. If there is no surplus income to pay other obligations, then bankruptcy should be considered not only by
the working debtor, but by the spouse, as well.

If the nonworking spouse fails to file, she may be held
accountable for some or all of the installment debts after
the husband has received his discharge. She would have
the right to petition the court for an order of contempt
against her ex-husband, because he has failed to pay the
bills pursuant to a divorce decree. However, since he was
absolved of the debts through bankruptcy, and chose this
route in order to pay alimony and support to the wife and
children, it is unlikely that the divorce court judge would

impose sanctions, even though he would have the right to do so.

It would be infinitely better for all concerned if both spouses joined in the bankruptcy to avoid the problem. This would stop all creditor pressure against both parties, and leave the husband free to concentrate on supporting himself and meeting his obligations for alimony and child support.

Are consumer bankruptcies more common than business bankruptcies?

More than 90 percent of the bankruptcies filed in the United States are consumer bankruptcies. But why not? There aren't as many businesses as there are consumers.

Do most people take bankruptcy too lightly?

Most people? Probably not. Of most of those who actually file, I would say, "Yes." There are about 250,000 cases filed annually, many if not most of them by debtors who could have dealt with their problems in less drastic ways. Personal bankruptcy is a very serious step to take to resolve one's financial problems, and it should be used only as a last resort. Serious legal ramifications can result from filing bankruptcy, and it is not without social implications, as well. Failure to make full disclosure of assets may result not only in a denial of the bankruptcy but in a federal criminal indictment that could lead to imprisonment.

Would it be better if all debtors decided never to file bankruptcy under any circumstances?

No, there are situations in which it is the only realistic choice. But its use should be limited to those situations;

other means should be used when they will solve the problem.

Is there any kind of insurance I can obtain when incurring a credit obligation that might protect me in the event I become disabled?

Yes, many lenders will arrange to have disability insurance provided under the contract, and add the premium to the installment balance. Credit life insurance is also available to pay the balance due on the loan in the event the debtor dies. Often, however, this insurance is unreasonably expensive, very profitable for the lender, and no more valuable than similar insurance coverage that can be obtained independent of the loan.

Will I lose all of my property if I file bankruptcy?

No. In fact, the exemptions provided in the bankruptcy reform act of 1978 are so generous that most debtors will probably be able to retain virtually everything they own. Each state allows different exemptions and the bankruptcy act also includes a list. Unless the state has a statute preventing the debtor from using the federal exemptions, he has a choice of electing use of either the state or the federal exemptions. The choice should be based on a determination of which offers the greatest advantage.

What property is exempted from liquidation under the federal statute?

First, the debtor gets an exemption of $7,500 worth of equity in his residence or personal property. If a husband and wife file jointly, $15,000 of value in these categories is automatically exempt. Each of them would also be allowed to keep $1,200 worth of equity in an automobile.

All items of household furnishings and similar personal property, up to a value of $200 per item, would be exempt. An aggregate value of $500 in personal jewelry of the debtor or a dependent and an aggregate value of $750 in professional books or tools of the trade of the debtor or a dependent is exempt. Even the cash value of life insurance policies, up to $4,000 for each debtor, is exempt.

If any items of personal property exceed the value allowed in the statute, they still may be claimed as exempt by applying a portion of the $7,500 allowance for real estate and personal property that is granted each debtor who files. This exemption can even be applied to cash that the debtor has on deposit in a bank account.

What type of income is protected under bankruptcy?

The federal act protects the debtor's right to receive a Social Security benefit, unemployment compensation, or a local public assistance benefit; a veterans' benefit; a disability, illness, or unemployment benefit; alimony, support, or separate maintenance, to the extent reasonably necessary for the support of the debtor and any dependent of the debtor; a payment under a stock bonus, pension, profit sharing, annuity, or similar plan or contract on account of illness, disability, death, age, or length of service, to the extent reasonably necessary for the support of the debtor and any dependent of the debtor, except in certain circumstances.

The act also protects the debtor's right to receive an award under a crime victim's reparation law; a payment on account of the wrongful death of an individual of whom the debtor was a dependent, to the extent reasonably necessary for the support of the debtor and any dependent of the debtor; a payment under a life insurance contract that insured the life of an individual of whom the debtor was a dependent on the date of such individual's death, to the extent reasonably necessary for the support of the debtor and any dependent of the debtor; a payment, not to exceed $7,500, on account of personal bodily injury, not including pain and suffering or compensation for actual pecuniary loss, of the debtor or an individual of whom the debtor is a dependent; or a payment in compensation of loss of future earnings of the debtor or an individual of whom the debtor is or was a dependent, to the extent reasonably necessary for the support of the debtor or a dependent of the debtor.

If I return household furnishings to the finance company that holds a security agreement, will bankruptcy discharge me from the obligation?

Yes, but there may be a more attractive alternative. The replacement cost of such items is always far in excess of their resale value as used merchandise. A better option, provided for in the bankruptcy act, would be to claim the furnishings as exempt personal property. A nonpossessory lien is not enforceable if it interferes with the debtor's right to an exemption under the bankruptcy act.

What about furniture that I bought on credit that is not yet paid for?

You may keep the furniture by agreeing to pay the creditor the current value, rather than the amount still owing.

I have a government insured student loan outstanding. Is this dischargeable in bankruptcy?

Only if it has been owing for more than five years or you can prove to the court that repayment would work a hardship on you and your dependents.

*I bought a car that turned out to be a lemon. I still owe
$5,000 on it. If I return the car to the finance company,
will I be released from the obligation?*

Under most state laws, returning the car forces the
finance company to sell the automobile to the highest
bidder and apply the funds received against the balance
you owe. They then have the right to demand the "deficiency balance" from you, unless deficiency balances have
been outlawed in your state. Sometimes the finance company, by agreement, will accept the return of the security
in satisfaction of the debt, but if they agree to do so, get it
in writing.

*The loan company that has taken my household goods
as security has been threatening to send out a truck to
repossess all of my furniture. Can they do this?*

Yes, they can, but they probably won't. In most cases
they use this only as a threat to extract payments. The
value of used furniture is probably not worth the cost of
picking it up. Further, the finance company is not in the
used furniture business and does not have the facilities to
dispose of used furniture. The best they could get would
be a tiny fraction of its cost. Actually, they lose the advantage if they actually do repossess because they will no
longer have the threat of doing so to use as leverage
against you.

*The company that financed my automobile is threaten-
ing to pick it up. Can they do so without a court order?*

Yes, in most states the right to repossess an automobile
upon default is a part of the contract. However, the finance company cannot do so unless you are willing to
give up the automobile. If you refuse to give it up and

keep it hidden, the finance company will have to go to court and secure an order to obtain possession of the automobile, after establishing that there is a default.

Can you still be held responsible for an obligation after a friend or relative has taken it over, made the payments for a time, and then defaulted?

Yes. Unless the original debtor has been released in writing by the seller, the creditor can look not only to the party assuming the debt, but also to the original party, once there is a default.

If there has been no crime involved, can a debtor go to jail for not paying his bills?

Debtor's prison has been abolished, but there is a procedure in some states called "citation to discover assets," wherein an order may be entered after judgment directing the debtor to make installment payments to the creditor. Failure to make the payments could subject the debtor to contempt of court proceedings for failure to comply with the court order. The judge could then find the debtor in contempt and order the debtor to jail, but exercise of this power by the state court is very rare.

I operated a small corporation that incurred a great deal of debt and finally was forced to go out of business. I have been advised to file a petition of bankruptcy in behalf of the corporation. There are no assets, so why is this action necessary?

Basically, it isn't, as long as the corporation, and not you as an individual, is the responsible party. Creditors could proceed against the corporation, but since it is out of business and there are no assets, they would be wasting their time and money in obtaining a judgment.

A problem for you will arise only if the creditors are suspicious that you or others in the operation may have converted corporate assets to your own personal use. Businessmen have been known to set up corporations to limit personal liability, and then use the assets improperly. Knowing this, creditors may attempt to "pierce the corporate veil" by going after the individual behind the corporate shell.

If they do, you may be burdened with substantial legal expenses in order to defend yourself. Consequently, it may be prudent to file bankruptcy in behalf of the corporation so that a full disclosure will be made to creditors. This probably will assure the creditors that you have nothing to hide. If you did—if you had converted corporate assets to your own use—it is not likely that you would file bankruptcy and give the judge, a trustee, and the creditors an opportunity to review your conduct in operating the corporation.

Does easy credit contribute to the large number of bankruptcies that are filed?

Of course. The easier credit is to obtain, and the greater the number of people who use it, the more bankruptcies there will be. This would be true if only the question of numbers were involved. The problem is compounded because, as the numbers increase, the quality of the debtors is reduced. Credit is extended to people who have little experience with it, who are not sophisticated in the management of their finances, who are imprudent in the purchases that they make, and who may have no compunctions about using credit to obtain merchandise they want, even though they know that they will never be able to pay.

If the bankruptcy rate continues to rise, will there be a definite impact on the economy?

If it rises high enough it may have some impact on the ease with which consumers can obtain credit. It is not likely, however, to have any impact on the solvency of the creditors. Despite the billions of dollars in outstanding consumer credit, and the number of bankruptcies that are filed, less than one percent of the outstanding consumer debt is charged off as uncollectible because of bankruptcy or simple inability of the borrower to pay.

The expectation of these losses is included in the finance charges and interest payments that are levied against the consumers who do pay their bills, and banking institutions maintain loan loss reserves to cover loans that go sour. Generally, it is only in cases of gross mismanagement that credit-grantors and lending institutions get in trouble because too many of their customers don't pay their bills.

20

Conclusion

Credit has become an essential element of our modern industrial society, and the pressure to use it has effected virtually every family in America. The tight-fisted and debt-fearing pioneers of an earlier time would find it difficult to comprehend a society in which futurists predict a day when money will all but disappear.

The use of credit has made a better life possible for most Americans, but inevitably there will be those for whom the consequences of credit become a nightmare from which society must provide an escape. True, those who use their credit privileges to willfully defraud creditors in order to indulge themselves in luxuries they cannot afford deserve little sympathy. But those who experience financial problems through no fault of their own should not feel stigmatized if they seek the protection that the Congress, in its wisdom, has concluded they deserve.

There will always be those who take advantage of the protection provided in the bankruptcy act and use it in ways that were not intended, for their own personal gain. But this is a small price for society to pay for the relief afforded others whose lives would be ruined if there were no way for them to escape their debts.

If you're in that position, don't be fearful or ashamed to see a lawyer who can put you on the road to your "fresh start."

Glossary

Automatic stay order under Chapter 13:   Similar to bank-ruptcy stay order, except that order remains in effect until all creditors are paid or plan is dismissed for nonpayment by debtor.

Bankruptcy discharge: Formal order entered by bank-ruptcy judge releasing the debtor from his debts.

Bankruptcy stay order: Automatic order becoming effec-tive upon filing of petition in bankruptcy to stop lawsuits, wage garnishment, or other forms of creditor harassment.

Budget analysis: Procedure used by Chapter 13 lawyer to determine whether a repayment plan is a possible financial solution; involves a study of all monthly income and fixed expenses to determine the amount of surplus income, if any, to be used for payment of creditors.

Claim: A right to payment or to an equitable remedy for breach of performance if such breach gives rise to a right to payment, whether or not such right is reduced to judgment, liquidated, unliquidated, fixed, contingent, matured, unmatured, disputed, undisputed, secured, or unsecured.

Collateral: Some security, in addition to the personal obligation of the borrower, usually in the form of a pledge of the debtor's furniture.

Composition plan: A repayment plan under the provisions of Chapter 13 of the Federal Bankruptcy Act in which creditors are offered an amount less than 100 percent of their claim.

Consolidation loan: Funds borrowed in order to retire many small obligations.

Consumer debt: Debt incurred by an individual primarily for personal, family, or household purposes.

Corporation: Includes: a) an association having a power or privilege that a private corporation, but not an individual or a partnership, possesses; b) a partnership association organized under a law that makes only the capital subscribed responsible for the debts of such association; c) a joint-stock company; d) an unincorporated company, association, or business trust. Does not include a limited partnership.

Creditor: a) an entity that has a claim against the debtor that arose at the time of or before the order for relief concerning the debtor; b) an entity that has a claim against the estate of the debtor; c) an entity that has a community claim.

Debt: Liability on a claim.

Debt pooler: A layman who, for a fee, contacts creditors and attempts to obtain each creditor's consent for a reduced payment without court supervision or protection.

Disinterested person: Generally, a person who is not a creditor of the debtor, and who has no pecuniary interest in the debtor's case.

Dunning notice: Generally, mailed reminders or threats of legal action unless scheduled payment is received.

Entity: A person, estate, trust, or governmental unit.

Equity interest: Value of property over and above the amount owed to a creditor holding security interest or lien.

Extension of debts: Plan under provisions of Chapter 13 wherein creditors are offered 100 percent of their claim over an extended period of time.

Federal Bankruptcy Act: A law for the benefit of debtors who are unable or unwilling to pay their debts.

Filing costs: Funds required by federal court clerk's office at time of filing of petition.

Individual with regular income: One whose income is sufficiently stable and regular enough to enable the individual to make payments under a plan under Chapter 13.

Insider: If the debtor is an individual, a relative of the debtor, or of a general partner of the debtor; a partnership in which the debtor is a general partner; a general partner of the debtor; a corporation of which the debtor is a director, officer, or person in control.

Insolvent: Generally, a condition in which the sum of an individual's debts is greater than the value of his property.

Judicial lien: A lien obtained by judgment, levy, sequestration, or other legal or equitable process or proceeding.

Legal aid bureau: Nonprofit organization offering free legal assistance to individuals or families who qualify.

Lien: Charge against or interest in property to secure payment of a debt or performance of an obligation.

Municipality: A political subdivision or public agency or instrumentality of a state.

Person: Includes an individual, partnership, or corporation, but not a governmental unit.

Personal bankruptcy—involuntary: Proceeding initiated by a creditor to adjudicate an individual a bankrupt without the debtor's consent.

Personal bankruptcy—voluntary: Proceeding initiated by the debtor's own petition to be adjudged a bankrupt and be released from obligations to creditors.

Reaffirmation agreement: Written promise to pay debt despite the release of the debt by a discharge in bankruptcy.

Relative: An individual related by affinity or consanguinity within the third degree as determined by the common law, or individual in a step or adoptive relationship within such third degree.

Secured creditors: Creditors who either retain title to goods in the debtor's possession or have some collateral in addition to the promise of the debtor, i.e., lien on debtor's household goods.

Secured debts: Obligations that are guaranteed by the pledge of debtor's personal property.

Security: Note; stock, treasury stock; bond; debenture; collateral trust certificate; preorganization certificate or subscription; transferable share; voting-trust certificate; certificate of deposit; certificate of deposit for security; investment contract or certificate of interest or participation in a profit-sharing agreement or in an oil, gas, or mineral royalty or lease, if such contract is the subject of a registration certificate with the SEC, or is exempt from filing; interest of a limited partner in a limited partnership; other claim or interest commonly known as "security"; certificate of interest or participation in, temporary or interim certificate for, receipt for, or warrant or right to subscribe to or purchase or sell, a security.

Security agreement: Form of financing agreement wherein the creditor retains title to property sold until purchase price is paid.

Security interest: Lien created by agreement.

Statutory lien: Lien arising solely by force of a statute on specified circumstances or conditions, or lien of distress for rent.

Straight bankruptcy: Proceeding in which debtor seeks to be relieved of financial obligations through liquidation of his nonexempt assets by a trustee, and disbursement of proceeds to creditors.

Trustee (Chapter 13): Court-appointed individual in Chapter 13 cases who collects payments from debtor and disburses them to creditors.

Unsecured debts: Personal obligations of borrower without any pledge of collateral.

Wage assignment: Agreement wherein debtor consents to his employer's deducting a portion of his wages each pay period for benefit of creditors.

Wage deduction order: Court order requiring employer to deduct a portion of debtor's wages for benefit of a particular creditor.

Appendix A:
List of bankruptcy trustees
and judges

Name of Trustee	Address	6/30/78 No. Cases Pending	Bankruptcy Judge
Alabama (middle)			
Richard E. Thompson	P.O. Box 173 Montgomery 36101	1866	Leon J. Hopper P.O. Box 1248 Montgomery 36102
Alabama (northern)			
Glen Andrews	P.O. Box 822 Anniston 36202	502	L. Chandler Watson P.O. Box 1805 Anniston 36201
Kathleen R. Miller	P.O. Box 847 Gadsden 35901	229	
J.C. Mahaffey	P.O. Box 1331 Decatur 35602	149	Edwin D. Breland P.O. Box 1289 Decatur 35601

161

Name of Trustee	Address	6/30/78 No. Cases Pending	Bankruptcy Judge
California (central)			
Elsie Davis	316 W. Second Street Suite 800 Los Angeles 90012	1265	Richard Mednick U.S. Courthouse 312 N. Spring St. Los Angeles 90012
Shannon J. Haney	2100 N. Broadway, #32 Santa Ana 92706	321	Peter M. Elliott 522 Federal Bldg. 34 Civic Center Plaza Santa Ana 92707
California (eastern)			
J. Roderick Jarrett	1410 Security Bank Bldg. Fresno 93721	363	Eckhart A. Thompson 4310 Federal Bldg. 1130 "O" Street Fresno 93721
Laurence Loheit	1020 Eighth Street Suite 307 Sacramento 95814	1540	Robert E. Woodward 8038 U.S. Courthouse 650 Capitol Mall Sacramento 95814
Jack A. Ulrich	P.O. Box 1114 930 Virginia Ave. Modesto 95353	100	Frederick W. Reyland, Jr. 2744 Second Street Ceres 95307
California (northern)			
Duncan H. Kester	P.O. Box 26800 San Jose 95159	1591	Warren C. Moore 209 U.S. P.O. Bldg. N. First & St. John Sts. San Jose 95113
Paul de Bruce Wolff	1212 Broadway Oakland 94612	1505	Cameron W. Wolfe P.O. Box 2070 214 Post Office Bldg. Oakland 94604
California (southern)			
Harry W. Heid	625 Broadway Room 514 San Diego 92101	1989	Ross M. Pyle U.S. Courthouse Fifth Floor San Diego 92101

Name of Trustee	Address	6/30/78 No. Cases Pending	Bankruptcy Judge
Colorado			
James E. Wagner	P.O. Box 1169 Denver 80201	813	John F. McGrath 1845 Sherman Street 400 Columbine Bldg. Denver 80203
Connecticut			
Joseph Neiman	171 Market Square Newington 06111	120	Saul Seidman 712 U.S. Courthouse 450 Main Street Hartford 06102
Herman S. Hodes	273 Orange Street New Haven 06510	3	
Arthur J. Gerstl	157 Golden Hill Street Bridgeport 06604	4	Robert E. Trevethan 319 U.S. Courthouse 915 Lafayette Blvd. Bridgeport 06604
Daniel Meister	71 East Avenue Norwalk 06851	7	
Delaware			
Mary S. Vendetti	P.O. Box 1470 Wilmington 19899	4	Helen S. Balick U.S. Courthouse 844 King Street Lockbox 38 Wilmington 19801
Marcia L. Pawlina	723 Philadelphia Pike Wilmington 19809	3	
District of Columbia			
Cynthia A. Niklas	Pitts, Wike, & Wingfield 1513 "P" Street, N.W. Washington 20005	26	Roger M. Whelan 2106 U.S. Courthouse Third & Constitution Washington 20001
Florida (middle)			
James A. Lenfestey	2306 Ardson Place Tampa 33609	6	Alexander L. Paskay P.O. Box 1198 Tampa 33601

Name of Trustee	Address	6/30/78 No. Cases Pending	Bankruptcy Judge
Florida (middle) continued			
Aaron Nathan	1892 Lake Spier Dr. Winter Park 32789	12	
Victor E. Raymos	205 Marine National Bank Bldg. Jacksonville 32202	8	George L. Proctor P.O. Box 485 240 U.S. P.O. & Courthouse 311 West Monroe St. Jacksonville 32201
Florida (southern)			
Jeanette E. Tavormina	1050 Seybold Bldg. Miami 33132	19	Thomas C. Britton P.O. Box 230 (33101) 14 N.E. First Ave. Miami 33132
Georgia (middle)			
Arthur E. Banks	Box 954 577 Mulberry Street Macon 31202	1204	W. Joseph Patterson, Jr. P.O. Box 90 126 U.S. Courthouse Mulberry and Third St. Macon 31202
Joe M. Flournoy	P.O. Box 5586 Columbus 31906	267	Algie M. Moseley, Jr. P.O. Box 2147 Columbus 31902
Georgia (northern)			
J. Sam Plowden	2410 Gas Light Tower Atlanta 30303	1701	Hugh Robinson, Jr. 309 U.S. Courthouse 56 Forsyth St. N.W. Atlanta 30303
Harmon T. Smith, Jr.	P.O. Box 1276 Gainesville 30501	16	
Donald C. Vanlandingham	P.O. Box 1963 Rome 30161	281	
Georgia (southern)			
Jack K. Berry	P.O. Box 9347 Savannah 31402	1154	Herman W. Coolidge P.O. Box 8347 Savannah 31402

Name of Trustee	Address	6/30/78 No. Cases Pending	Bankruptcy Judge
Hawaii			
Yee Hee	Merchandise Mart Bldg. Room 329 198 S. Hotel Street Honolulu 96813	51	Jon J. Chinen P.O. Box 50121 Honolulu 96850
Idaho			
Lois A. Christy	4485 Adams St. Boise 83704	393	Merlin S. Young P.O. Box 2755 Eighth & Bannock Sts. Boise 83701
L.D. Fitzgerald	P.O. Box 2071 Pocatello 83201	209	
L.C. Spurgeon	Box 820 Coeur d'Alene 83814	99	
Eileene Whiteley	P.O. Box 211 Oakley 83346	16	
Illinois (eastern)			
Glen R. Barmann	1113 E. Court Street Kankakee 60901	7	Larry L. Lessen P.O. Box 585 Danville 61832
John Tierney	41 on the Mall Danville 61832	5	
James W. McRoberts, Jr.	8787 State Street Room 200 E. St. Louis 62203	94	James D. Trabue P.O. Box 386 E. St. Louis 62202
Illinois (northern)			
James E. Kohlhorst	1515 Windsor Road Loves Park 61111	474	Richard N. DeGunther 211 S. Court St. Rockford 61104
Craig Phelps	53 W. Jackson Blvd. Chicago 60604	4853	Richard L. Merrick U.S. Courthouse 219 S. Dearborn St. Chicago 60604

Name of Trustee	Address	6/30/78 No. Cases Pending	Bankruptcy Judge
Indiana (southern) continued			
Harry C. Dees, Jr.	28 South 5th St. Terre Haute 47807	25	
Raymond B. Woodward	155 E. Main St. New Albany 47150	22	
Robert A. Brothers	21 N. Pennsylvania 3rd Floor Indianapolis 46204	4	Robert L. Bayt 317 A U.S. Courthouse Indianapolis 46204
A. Thomas Cobb	1314 First Federal Bldg. Indianapolis 46204	8	Richard W. Vandivier 320 U.S. Courthouse Indianapolis 46204
Paul Hirsch	1815 North Meridian St. Indianapolis 46202		
Thomas C. Tumbove	700 King Cole Bldg. 7 N. Meridian St. Indianapolis 46204	7	Nicholas Sufana 318 U.S. Courthouse Indianapolis 46204
Iowa (northern)			
W. J. Giles, III	722 Frances Bldg. Sioux City 51101	22	William W. Thinnes P.O. Box 4371 Cedar Rapids 52407
Larry G. Gutz	2720 First Ave. N.E. P.O. Box 1943 Cedar Rapids 52406	59	
Iowa (southern)			
Richard A. Bowers	1800 Third Ave. Rock Island, Ill. 61201	161	Richard F. Stageman 318 U.S. Courthouse Des Moines 50309
Dale E. Maron	509 West Broadway Council Bluffs 51501	9	
F. M. McCormick	517 Fifth St. Des Moines 50309	60	
Kansas			
Joseph H. McDowell	334 Brotherhood Bldg. Kansas City 66101	750	Benjamin E. Franklin P.O. Box 1339 Kansas City 66117

Name of Trustee	Address	6/30/78 No. Cases Pending	Bankruptcy Judge
Kansas continued			
James L. Quinn	400 Kansas Ave. Lower L Five Topeka 66603	238	James A. Pusateri Room 319 U.S. Courthouse Topeka 66603
Royce E. Wallace	328 North Main Suite 200 Wichita 67202	547	Robert B. Morton P.O. Box 1881 Wichita 67201
Kentucky (eastern)			
Sidney N. White	111 Church St. Lexington 40507	697	Joe Lee P.O. Box 1079 Lexington 40501
Kentucky (western)			
G. William Brown	436 S. Seventh St. Louisville 40202	473	Merritt S. Deitz 414 U.S. Courthouse Sixth and Broadway Louisville 40202
Louisiana (eastern)			
Lloyd A. Pizzaloto, Sr.	410/411 Masonic Temple Bldg. 333 St. Charles St. New Orleans 70130	296	Thomas M. Brahney, III U.S. Courthouse 500 Camp St. New Orleans 70130
Louisiana (western)			
S.S. Holland, Jr.	P.O. Box 1108 Lake Charles 70602	14	Francis R. Bernard, Jr. P.O. Box 71 Opelousas 70570
Emile C. Toups	P.O. Box 3264 Lafayette 70502	11	
E.W. Holloway	1816 Jackson St. Alexandria 71301	140	
E.F. Longridge	P.O. Box 5091 3331 Youree Dr. Shreveport 71105	393	
John C. Massey	P.O. Box 2616 Monroe 71207	32	

Name of Trustee	Address	6/30/78 No. Cases Pending	Bankruptcy Judge
Michigan (western) continued			
Philip A. Brown	600 Main St. St. Joseph 49085	10	
Maurice A. Edleman	409-C Waters Bldg. Grand Rapids 49503	16	
Donald W. Kreling	1003 Roseland Ave. Kalamazoo 49001	87	
Edward M. Yampolsky	2162 Broadway Benton Harbor 49022	9	
Minnesota			
Albert E. Baddin	401 Providence Bldg. Duluth 55802	5	Patrick J. McNulty 412 U.S. P.O. & Courthouse Duluth 55802
J. J. Mickelson	107 Upper Midwest Bldg. Minneapolis 55401	1363	Kenneth G. Owens 550 U.S. Courthouse 110 S. Fourth St. Minneapolis 55401
Mississippi (northern)			
Jacob C. Pongetti	126 Fifth St., N. Columbus 39701	3	Eugene J. Raphael P.O. Box 1558 618 Washington Ave. Greenville 38701
Mississippi (southern)			
Robert R. Marshall	1440 Deposit Guaranty Plaza Jackson 39201	26	Barney E. Eaton, III P.O. Drawer 2448 Jackson 39205
J. C. Bell	P.O. Box 566 Hattiesburg 39401	3	
Missouri (eastern)			
Edward J. Karfeld	611 Olive St. Suite 2020 St. Louis 63101	7	James J. Barta 730 U.S. Courthouse 1114 Market St. St. Louis 63101

Name of Trustee	Address	6/30/78 No. Cases Pending	Bankruptcy Judge
Missouri (eastern) continued			
Eileen Voss	7711 Carondelet Clayton 63105	4	Robert E. Brauer 730 U.S. Courthouse 1114 Market St. St. Louis 63101
Missouri (western)			
Betty Clair	905 Ozark National Life Bldg. 906 Grand Ave. Kansas City 64106	1627	Jack C. Jones 919 U.S. Courthouse 801 Grand Ave. Kansas City 64106
Nebraska			
Kenneth E. Shreves	802 Omaha Grain Exchange Bldg. Omaha 68102	295	David L. Crawford P.O. Box 1197 9015 New Federal Bldg. Omaha 68101
Nevada			
Hugh P. Hough	3421 E. Tonopah Ave. N. Las Vegas 89030	21	Lloyd D. George P.O. Box 16018 Las Vegas 89101
William Van Arsdale	4035 Jasper Lane Reno 89509	6	Bert Goldwater 4050 Federal Bldg. and Courthouse 300 Booth St. Reno 89502
New Jersey			
David A. Kasen	807 Haddon Ave. Haddonfield 08033	68	William Lipkin P.O. Box 1465 U.S. Courthouse & P.O. Bldg. 401 Market St. Camden 08101
Theodore Meth	P.O. Box 1013 Mountainside 07092	200	Amel Stark P.O. Box 1388 Trenton 08607

Name of Trustee	Address	6/30/78 No. Cases Pending	Bankruptcy Judge
New Mexico			
Bruce C. Redd	420 Sandia Savings Bldg. Albuquerque 87102	87	Robert A. Johnson P.O. Box 546 Albuquerque 87103
New York (eastern)			
William S. Brown	261 Broadway New York 10007	8	Boris Radoyevich 900 Ellison Ave. Westbury 11590
Bertram J. Berger	276 Fifth Ave. New York 10001	58	
Robert W. Tauber	26 Court St. Brooklyn 11242	8	Manuel J. Price U.S. Courthouse 225 Cadman Plaza, E. 35 Tillary St. Brooklyn 11201
New York (northern)			
Warren V. Blasland	600 Monroe Bldg. Syracuse 13202	8	Leon J. Marketos 311 U.S. Courthouse Utica 31503
Leon J. Debernardis	288 Genesee St. Utica 13502	7	
New York (western)			
Albert J. Mogravero	Room 1202 69 Delaware Ave. Buffalo 14202	1009	John W. Creahan 312 U.S. Courthouse Niagara Square Buffalo 14202
Robert T. Cryan	Room 1202 69 Delaware Ave. Buffalo 14202	1493	
New York (southern)			
Bertram J. Berger	276 Fifth Avenue New York 10001	30	Roy Babitt 230 U.S. Courthouse Foley Square New York 10007

Name of Trustee	Address	6/30/78 No. Cases Pending	Bankruptcy Judge
North Carolina (eastern)			
Trawick H. Stubbs, Jr.	P.O. Box 1654 318 Craven St. New Bern 28560	508	Thomas M. Moore P.O. Box 695 309 Green St. Wilson 27893
Malcolm J. Howard	P.O. Box 859 Greenville 27834	468	
North Carolina (middle)			
Richard D. Sparkman	Suite 300, Liberty Walk N.C. National Bank Plaza Winston-Salem 27701	597	Rufus W. Reynolds P.O. Drawer C-2 418 U.S. P.O. & Courthouse 324 Market St. Greensboro 27402
Richard M. Hutson, II	306 Allentown Bldg. 119 Orange St. Durham 27710	627	
Anita J. Kinlaw	224 Commerce Place Greensboro 27402	1166	
North Carolina (western)			
Robert M. Burroughs	901 Elizabeth Ave. Charlotte 28204	1266	Marvin R. Wooten P.O. Box 1109 209 P.O. Bldg. 401 West Trade St. Charlotte 28231
North Dakota			
James H. Herzog	P.O. Box 3045 Fargo 58102	20	Gordon Thompson P.O. Box 1110 Fargo 58102
Ohio (northern)			
Anthony B. Disalle	201 Security Bldg. Toledo 43604	133	Richard L. Speer 113 U.S. Courthouse 1716 Spielbusch Ave. Toledo 43624

Name of Trustee	Address	6/30/78 No. Cases Pending	Bankruptcy Judge
Ohio (northern) continued			
Robert N. Heller	280 N. Park Ave. Warren 44482	47	Joseph T. Molitoris 301-306 U.S. P.O. & Courthouse Youngstown 44501
Jerome L. Holub	1113 Centran Bldg. Akron 44308	526	Harold F. White U.S. Courthouse & Federal Bldg. Akron 44308
Alton L. Rinier	704 Peoples Merchant Trust Bldg. Canton 44702	832	James H. Williams 640 Citizens Bldg. 100 Central Plaza, S. Canton 44702
Myron E. Wasserman	901 Bond Court Bldg. Cleveland 44114	85	John F. Ray, Jr. Federal Bldg. Public Square Cleveland 44114
Ohio (southern)			
Arthur C. Elliott	306 26 East Sixth St. Cincinnati 45202	1577	Leonard C. Gartner 725 U.S. Courthouse Fifth and Walnut Sts. Cincinnati 45202
Frank Pees	5878 High St. Worthington 43085	487	Robert J. Sidman 149 U.S. Courthouse 85 Marconi Blvd. Columbus 43215
O. J. Gerhardstein	200 West Second St. Dayton 45402	47	Ellis W. Kerr Federal Bldg. & U.S. Courthouse 200 W. Dayton St. Dayton 45402
Oklahoma (northern)			
Fred W. Woodson	1640 South Boston Ave. Tulsa 74119	31	William E. Rutledge 4-540 U.S. Courthouse Tulsa 74103

Name of Trustee	Address	6/30/78 No. Cases Pending	Bankruptcy Judge
South Dakota			
Robert J. Kean	8702 National Bank Bldg. of South Dakota Sioux Falls 57102	6	Peder K. Ecker Suite 517 101 S. Main Sioux Falls 57102
Tennessee (eastern)			
Tate E. Carty	1020 United American Bldg. Knoxville 37902	115	Clive W. Bare P.O. Box 1189 220 Federal Bldg. Knoxville 37901
Frank D. Gibson	110 E. Market Street Kingsport 37660	37	
C. Kenneth Still	18 Patten Parkway P.O. Box 305 Chattanooga 37401	1422	Ralph H. Kelley P.O. Box 1189 Chattanooga 37401
Tennessee (middle)			
James L. Beckner	P.O. Box 2601 Nashville 37219	532	Paul E. Jennings U.S. Courthouse 801 Broadway Nashville 37203
Tennessee (western)			
Mrs. B.S. Chism	Room 214 Federal Bldg. Memphis 38103	2893	Odell D. Horton Federal Bldg. 167 N. Main Street Memphis 38103
John Van Den Bosch	107 S. Shannon Jackson 38301	174	
Texas (northern)			
Carl S. Fitzgerald	2430 One Main Place Dallas 75250	7	Dean M. Gandy Federal Bldg. and Courthouse 1100 Commerce Street Dallas 75242
Clifford F. McMaster	1702 Commerce Bank Bldg. Ft. Worth 76102	3	Ernest J. Flowers 206 U.S. Courthouse Fort Worth 76102

Name of Trustee	Address	6/30/78 No. Cases Pending	Bankruptcy Judge
Virginia (western)			
Ernest L. Light	P.O. 2256 Roanoke 24009	287	H. Clyde Pearson P.O. Box 2390 3rd Floor New Federal Bldg. 2nd St. and Franklin Road. S.W. Roanoke 24010
James E. Nunley	Box 117 Bristol 24201	262	
Melba C. Pirkey	P.O. Box 1205 Roanoke 24006	498	
John G. Leake	Box 526 Harrisonburg 22801	87	Thomas J. Wilson P.O. Box 586 310 Federal Bldg. Harrisonburg 22801
James Goodson, III	726 Masonic Bldg. Danville 24541	175	Philip H. Hickson 205 Federal Bldg. Lynchburg 24505
Emily Y. Wilson	211 Fifth Street, N.E. Charlottesville 22901	74	
E.F. Younger, Jr.	P.O. Box 1037 915½ Main Street Lynchburg 24505	598	
Washington (eastern)			
P.R. Derr	326 P.O. Bldg. P.O. Box 2212 Spokane 99210	605	L. Warden Hanel P.O. Box 2164 Spokane 99210
Washington (western)			
Virginia Petta	P.O. Box 1106 1413 Fourteenth Ave. Longview 98632	352	Robert W. Skidmore 224 P.O. Bldg. Tacoma 98402
Keith B. Overhansly	413 Washington Blvd. Tacoma 98402	767	

Name of Trustee	Address	6/30/78 No. Cases Pending	Bankruptcy Judge
Washington (western) continued			
Irwin Kleinman	505 Madison St. Seattle 90104	787	Sidney C. Volinn 220 U.S. Courthouse Fifth & Madison Sts. Seattle 98104
West Virginia (northern)			
James J. Harkins	1 Thirteenth St. Wheeling 26003	5	John H. Kamlowsky P.O. Box 70 (26003) 322 Federal Bldg. & Courthouse 12th & Chapline Sts. Wheeling 26004
West Virginia (southern)			
John N. Charnock, Jr.	P.O. Box 207 Charleston 25321	—	Edwin F. Flowers 4402 U.S. Courthouse 500 Quarrier St. Charleston 25301
Wisconsin (eastern)			
Raymond Burczyk	313 Sixth St. Racine 53403	127	Dale E. Ihlenfeldt 333 Federal Bldg. 517 E. Wisconsin Ave. Milwaukee 53202
Joseph G. Koll	19 East First St. Fond du Lac 54935	41	Howard W. Hilgendorf 333 Federal Bldg. 517 E. Wisconsin Ave. Milwaukee 53202
Marjorie L. Marshall	110 E. Wisconsin Ave. Milwaukee 53202	460	Dale E. Ihlenfeldt 33 Federal Bldg. 517 E. Wisconsin Ave. Milwaukee 53202
Wisconsin (western)			
William A. Chatterton	P.O. Box 631 324 S. Hamilton Madison 53701	323	Robert D. Martin P.O. Box 548 Madison 53701

Name of Trustee	Address	6/30/78 No. Cases Pending	Bankruptcy Judge
Wyoming			
John H. Drew	816 E. Prosser Rd. Cheyenne 82001	13	Harold L. Mai P.O. Box 1107 New Post Office and Courthouse 2120 Capitol Ave. Cheyenne 82001

Appendix B:
Chapter 13 forms

The following are reproductions of the official forms for use in filing Chapter 13 cases under the new Federal Bankruptcy Code. They include an application to pay filing fees in installments, a Chapter 13 statement, a monthly family budget, a schedule of debts, a list of property owned by the debtor, and an exemptions form. These forms should give you an idea of what to expect should you ever elect to file under Chapter 13.

184

United States Bankruptcy Court

IN RE:

_____
Case Number

APPLICATION TO PAY FILING FEES IN INSTALLMENTS

1. The applicant is filing herewith a petition and a plan under Chapter 13 of Title 11 of the United States Code.

2. The applicant is unable to pay all (or a part) of the filing fees except in installments and propose that such fees be paid to the Chapter 13 Trustee in the installments as proposed in the plan filed herewith.

3. No money has been paid to the applicant's attorney for services in connection with this case or with any pending case under said Title 11 and no payment will be made to the attorney for such services except through the Trustee in this case.

WHEREFORE applicant prays for permission to pay all or the balance of the filing fees in installments.

_____
DATE

_____
APPLICANT

_____
APPLICANT

ORDER PERMITTING PAYMENT OF FILING FEES IN INSTALLMENTS

The foregoing application having been considered:

It is ordered that the debtor pay any filing fee still owing by paying to the Chapter 13 Trustee the installment payments proposed in the debtor's plan; and

It is further ordered that the debtor shall pay no money and shall transfer no property to the attorney for services in connection with this case except as may be allowed by the court and paid by the Trustee pursuant to the plan and the orders of this court; and

It is further ordered that the debtor's attorney shall accept no money or property from the debtor or his spouse for services in connection with this case or any pending case under Title 11 of the United States Code, and that any award of compensation to the attorney for services in connection with this case shall be governed by such title and the Rules promulgated pursuant thereto.

_____
DATE

_____
BANKRUPTCY JUDGE

APPROVED _____
ATTORNEY FOR APPLICANT(S)

United States Bankruptcy Court

IN RE: (If a joint petition use both names.)

NAME	SSN

NAME	SSN

	NUMBER

POST
OFFICE
ADDRESS

COUNTY OF RESIDENCE _____

Other names used by the petitioner(s) within the past 6 years.

ORIGINAL PETITION AND PLAN
UNDER CHAPTER 13, TITLE 11 of the UNITED STATES CODE

All references herein to the Petitioner or the Debtor will be made using the singular masculine gender even though the actual reference may be to a female petitioner or to joint petitioners.

Petitioner is an individual, not a stockbroker or a commodity broker, whose income is sufficiently stable to enable your petitioner to make payments under a plan under Chapter 13 of Title 11 U.S.C., who owes noncontingent, liquidated, unsecured debts aggregating less than $100,000.00 and noncontingent, liquidated, secured debts of less than $350,000.00.

The petitioner's domicile, residence, principal place of business or principal assets (or one of them) are or have been in this district for a longer portion of the preceeding 180 days than in any other district.

Wherefore petitioner prays for relief under Chapter 13 of Title 11 U.S.C., and proposes a plan as follows:

1. The debtor submits all, or such portion of his future earnings or other future income to the control of the trustee as is necessary for the execution of the plan.

2. All claims entitled to priority under 11 U.S.C. ¶ 507 shall be paid in full in deferred cash payments as provided on the attached Schedule of Debts, unless the holder of a particular claim agrees to a different treatment of such claim.

3. Other claims duly filed and allowed or deemed allowed shall be discharged by payment to the extent, in the manner and order of priority as indicated on the attached "Schedule of Debts".

CERTIFICATION OF PETITION AND ATTACHED CHAPTER 13 STATEMENT

Each of the undersigned states under penalties of perjury that he has read the foregoing petition, plan and the attached Chapter 13 statement consisting of _____ pages and that the matters therein stated and the answers given are true and complete to the best of my knowledge, information and belief.

_____
PETITIONER

_____
PETITIONER

APPLICATION FOR ALLOWANCE AND DISCLOSURE OF COMPENSATION PAID OR PROMISED TO ATTORNEY FOR DEBTOR
Application is hereby made for an allowance of reasonable compensation to be paid in by or for the debtor under the provisions of the proposed plan.

The compensation paid or promised or property transferred or promised to the undersigned as compensation for services rendered or to be rendered in connection with this case other than that to be allowed by the court and paid by the trustee. is indicated in the Chapter 13 statement filed herewith. Except only as may be specially noted hereon. I have not shared or agreed to share such compensation (either paid or to be paid) with any other person other than with members or regular associates of the law firm with which I am associated.

ATTORNEY FOR PETITIONER:

_____
SIGNATURE

NAME, ADDRESS & TELEPHONE NO.

PETITION AND PLAN

187

CHAPTER 13 STATEMENT

NAME OF DEBTOR _____

EACH QUESTION SHOULD BE ANSWERED OR THE FAILURE TO ANSWER EXPLAINED. IF ADDITIONAL SPACE IS NEEDED FOR THE ANSWER TO ANY QUESTION, A SEPARATE SHEET, PROPERLY IDENTIFIED AND MADE A PART HEREOF, SHOULD BE USED AND ATTACHED.

(IF THE ANSWER TO A SPOUCE'S QUESTION IS THE SAME AS FOR THE DEBTOR, THE QUESTION MAY BE ANSWERED "SAME")

QUESTIONS TO BE ANSWERED BY THE DEBTOR	QUESTIONS TO BE ANSWERED BY THE SPOUSE, IF ANY (IF DEBTOR IS UNMARRIED OR SEPARATED, SO STATE)
WHAT DO YOU CONSIDER YOUR PERMANENT RESIDENCE IF DIFFERENT FROM THAT LISTED ABOVE?	WHAT DO YOU CONSIDER YOUR PERMANENT RESIDENCE IF DIFFERENT FROM THAT LISTED ABOVE?
TELEPHONE NO.	TELEPHONE NO.
GIVE PRESENT OCCUPATION (IF MORE THAN ONE, LIST ALL)	GIVE PRESENT OCCUPATION (IF MORE THAN ONE, LIST ALL)
PRESENT EMPLOYER: STREET ADDRESS CITY & STATE	PRESENT EMPLOYER: STREET ADDRESS CITY & STATE
TELEPHONE NO. _____ BADGE OR EMPLOYEE NO	TELEPHONE NO. _____ BADGE OR EMPLOYEE NO.
HOW LONG HAVE YOU BEEN EMPLOYED BY THIS EMPLOYER?	HOW LONG HAVE YOU BEEN EMPLOYED BY THIS EMPLOYER?
IF YOU HAVE NOT BEEN EMPLOYED BY YOUR PRESENT EMPLOYER FOR A PERIOD OF ONE YEAR STATE THE NAME OF PRIOR EMPLOYER(S) AND NATURE OF EMPLOYMENT DURING THAT PERIOD.	IF YOU HAVE NOT BEEN EMPLOYED BY YOUR PRESENT EMPLOYER FOR A PERIOD OF ONE YEAR STATE THE NAME OF PRIOR EMPLOYER(S) AND NATURE OF EMPLOYMENT DURING THAT PERIOD.

HOW OFTEN ARE YOU PAID AND WHAT ARE YOUR GROSS WAGES, SALARY OR COMMISSIONS DUE EACH TIME?

WEEKLY ☐   SEMI-MONTHLY ☐   MONTHLY ☐   OTHER ☐

GROSS WAGES $ ☐

PAYROLL DEDUCTIONS:
WITHHOLDING & SOC. SEC. TAXES $ _____

INSURANCE $ _____

CREDIT UNION $ _____

UNION DUES $ _____

OTHER $ _____

NET TAKE HOME PAY $ ☐

IF YOUR EMPLOYMENT IS SUBJECT TO SEASONAL OR OTHER CHANGES INDICATE THE IDLE SEASON

HAVE YOU OPERATED A BUSINESS IN PARTNERSHIP OR OTHERWISE DURING THE PAST THREE YEARS? (IF SO, GIVE THE PARTICULARS, INCLUDING NAMES, DATES AND PLACES).

IF YOU OPERATE A BUSINESS OR PROFESSION INDICATE THE NATURE THEREOF. THE AMOUNT AND FREQUENCY OF THE INCOME AVAILABLE FOR THE PURPOSE OF MAKING PAYMENTS UNDER A PLAN, AND ATTACH A STATEMENT OF AFFAIRS FOR A DEBTOR ENGAGED IN BUSINESS.

WHAT WAS THE AMOUNT OF YOUR GROSS INCOME FOR THE LAST CALENDAR YEAR? $ _____

HAVE YOU MADE ANY WAGE ASSIGNMENT OR ALLOTMENT (IF SO, INDICATE THE PERSON TO WHOM ASSIGNED - FULL NAME AND ADDRESS SHOULD BE ON LIST OF CREDITORS).

HOW OFTEN ARE YOU PAID AND WHAT ARE YOUR GROSS WAGES, SALARY OR COMMISSIONS DUE EACH TIME?

WEEKLY ☐   SEMI-MONTHLY ☐   MONTHLY ☐   OTHER ☐

GROSS WAGES $ ☐

PAYROLL DEDUCTIONS:
WITHHOLDING & SOC. SEC. TAXES $ _____

INSURANCE $ _____

CREDIT UNION $ _____

UNION DUES $ _____

OTHER $ _____

NET TAKE HOME PAY $ ☐

IF YOUR EMPLOYMENT IS SUBJECT TO SEASONAL OR OTHER CHANGES INDICATE THE IDLE SEASON

HAVE YOU OPERATED A BUSINESS IN PARTNERSHIP OR OTHERWISE DURING THE PAST THREE YEARS? (IF SO, GIVE THE PARTICULARS, INCLUDING NAMES, DATES AND PLACES).

IF YOU OPERATE A BUSINESS OR PROFESSION INDICATE THE NATURE THEREOF. THE AMOUNT AND FREQUENCY OF THE INCOME AVAILABLE FOR THE PURPOSE OF MAKING PAYMENTS UNDER A PLAN, AND ATTACH A STATEMENT OF AFFAIRS FOR A DEBTOR ENGAGED IN BUSINESS.

WHAT WAS THE AMOUNT OF YOUR GROSS INCOME FOR THE LAST CALENDAR YEAR? $ _____

HAVE YOU MADE ANY WAGE ASSIGNMENT OR ALLOTMENT (IF SO, INDICATE THE PERSON TO WHOM ASSIGNED - FULL NAME AND ADDRESS SHOULD BE ON LIST OF CREDITORS).

190

NAME OF DEBTOR _____

MONTHLY FAMILY BUDGET

EXPENSES

GIVE ESTIMATED AVERAGE FUTURE MONTHLY EXPENSES OF FAMILY
(NOT INCLUDING DEBTS TO BE PAID UNDER PLAN) CONSISTING OF

RENT OR HOME LOAN PAYMENT
(INCLUDE LOT RENTED FOR MOBILE HOME) .... $ _____

UTILITIES
- ELECTRICITY $ _____
- WATER $ _____
- HEAT $ _____
- TELEPHONE $ _____
- OTHER $ _____

TOTAL UTILITIES $ _____

FOOD $ _____

CLOTHING $ _____

LAUNDRY & CLEANING $ _____

NEWSPAPERS, PERIODICALS & BOOKS (INCLUDING SCHOOL BOOKS) $ _____

DOCTOR & MEDICAL EXPENSES $ _____

TRANSPORTATION (NOT INCLUDING AUTO PAYMENTS TO BE PAID UNDER PLAN) $ _____

RECREATION, CLUB & ENTERTAINMENT $ _____

INCOME

GIVE ESTIMATED AVERAGE FUTURE MONTHLY INCOME CONSISTING OF:

DEBTOR'S TAKE HOME PAY (PER MONTH) _____

SPOUSE'S TAKE HOME PAY (PER MONTH) _____

REGULAR INCOME AVAILABLE FROM
OPERATION OF BUSINESS OR PROFESSION _____

DO YOU RECEIVE ANY ALIMONY OR SUPPORT PAYMENTS?
IF SO, STATE MONTHLY AMOUNT $ _____

THE NAME, AGE & RELATIONSHIP TO YOU OF PERSONS FOR
WHOSE BENEFIT PAYMENTS ARE RECEIVED.

PENSION, SOCIAL SECURITY OR RETIREMENT INCOME _____

OTHER MONTHLY INCOME _____

TOTAL MONTHLY INCOME _____

INSURANCE (NOT DEDUCTED FROM WAGES)

AUTO $ ___

LIFE $ ___

OTHER $ ___

TOTAL INSURANCE $ ___

TAXES NOT DEDUCTED FROM WAGES OR INCLUDED IN HOME LOAN PAYMENTS

IF YOU PAY OR ARE LIABLE FOR PAYMENT OF ALIMONY OR SUPPORT PAYMENTS.

IF SO, STATE MONTHLY AMOUNT $ ___

THE NAME, AGE & RELATIONSHIP TO YOU OF PERSONS FOR WHOSE BENEFIT PAYMENTS ARE MADE.

TOTAL MONTHLY EXPENSES ___

AMT OF PLAN PAYMENT TO THE TRUSTEE ___

TOTAL OF EXPENSES AND PLAN PAYMENT

DIFFERENCE ___

DEPENDENTS

NUMBER, AGE & RELATIONSHIP OF DEPENDENTS (EXCEPT CURRENT SPOUSE)

PAYMENTS FOR SUPPORT OF ADDITIONAL DEPENDENTS NOT LIVING AT YOUR HOME. $ ___

OTHER (EXPLAIN) $ ___

TOTAL ESTIMATED FUTURE MONTHLY EXPENSES $ ___

COMPENSATION PAID OR PROMISED TO ATTORNEY FOR DEBTOR

HAVE YOU PAID OR AGREED TO PAY (OR TRANSFERED OR AGREED TO TRANSFER ANY PROPERTY) TO YOUR ATTORNEY FOR SERVICES IN CONNECTION WITH YOUR CASE OTHER THAN AGREEING TO PAY SUCH COMPENSATION AS MAY BE ALLOWED BY THE COURT TO BE PAID BY THE TRUSTEE FROM MONIES PAID TO THE TRUSTEE FOR YOUR ACCOUNT?   YES ☐   NO ☐

IF THE ANSWER IS YES, STATE THE NATURE AND THE AMOUNT OF COMPENSATION PAID OR PROMISED AND THE SOURCE OF THE PAYMENT.

SCHEDULE OF DEBTS
and
DEBTOR'S PROPOSED PLAN OF DEALING WITH CREDITORS

After the payment of the costs of administration as provided by order of the court, the moneys paid to the trustee shall be distributed as indicated on this schedule of debts.

Specific or fixed monthly payments to certain creditors, if any, are noted opposite the name and address of the creditor or creditors to receive such specific payment or payments. The remaining funds shall be paid to all other creditors in a manner that provides the same treatment for each claim within a particular class. In no event shall the amount to be distributed to each creditor under the plan be less than the value (as of the effective date of the plan) of the property upon which such creditor had an enforceable lien, plus the amount, if any, that would be paid such claim if the estate of the debtor were to liquidated under chapter 7 of Title 11 of the United States Code.

With respect to each allowed secured claim the Plan is intended to comply with the requirements of 11 USC 1325(a) (5) (A and B) and unless otherwise specifically noted on the attached "Schedule of Debts" the Plan does not propose that the debtor surrender any property to the holders of secured claims.

Indicate in "Remarks" if the claim is:
  1. Disputed Contingent or Unliquidated.
  2. Subject to a Setoff.
  3. Evidenced By a Judgment. (If so, identify the case).
  4. A Claim Incurred as a Partner, Joint Contractor or
     Consigner. (if so, identify the entity).

NAME, ADDRESS, ZIP CODE AND ACCOUNT NO. IF ANY. State the name of Creditor (including the last known holder of any negotiable instrument) and the residence or place of business of each creditor (if unknown, so state).	AMOUNT DUE OR CLAIMED BY CREDITOR	CLASSIFICATION OR CODES	MONTHLY PAYMENTS DUE PER CONTRACT	NUMBER OF INSTALLMENTS IN ARREARS	SPECIFIC PAYMENTS, IF ANY TO BE MADE UNDER THE DEBTOR'S PLAN	MONTHLY PAYMENTS PROPOSED BY THE PLAN
	IF DISPUTED, AMT. ADMITTED	BRIEF DESCRIPTION OF SECURITY IF ANY				
1						

REMARKS:

NAME, ADDRESS, ZIP CODE AND ACCOUNT NO. IF ANY	AMOUNT DUE OR CLAIMED BY CREDITOR	CLASSIFICATION OR CODES	MONTHLY PAYMENTS DUE PER CONTRACT	NUMBER OF INSTALLMENTS IN ARREARS	MONTHLY PAYMENTS PROPOSED BY THE PLAN
	IF DISPUTED. AMT. ADMITTED	BRIEF DESCRIPTION OF SECURITY IF ANY			

2

REMARKS:

NAME, ADDRESS, ZIP CODE AND ACCOUNT NO. IF ANY	AMOUNT DUE OR CLAIMED BY CREDITOR	CLASSIFICATION OR CODES	MONTHLY PAYMENTS DUE PER CONTRACT	NUMBER OF INSTALLMENTS IN ARREARS	MONTHLY PAYMENTS PROPOSED BY THE PLAN
	IF DISPUTED. AMT. ADMITTED	BRIEF DESCRIPTION OF SECURITY IF ANY			

3

REMARKS:

NAME, ADDRESS, ZIP CODE AND ACCOUNT NO. IF ANY	AMOUNT DUE OR CLAIMED BY CREDITOR	CLASSIFICATION OR CODES	MONTHLY PAYMENTS DUE PER CONTRACT	NUMBER OF INSTALLMENTS IN ARREARS	MONTHLY PAYMENTS PROPOSED BY THE PLAN
	IF DISPUTED. AMT. ADMITTED	BRIEF DESCRIPTION OF SECURITY IF ANY			

4

REMARKS:

NAME, ADDRESS, ZIP CODE AND ACCOUNT NO. IF ANY	AMOUNT DUE OR CLAIMED BY CREDITOR	CLASSIFICATION OR CODES	MONTHLY PAYMENTS DUE PER CONTRACT	NUMBER OF INSTALLMENTS IN ARREARS	MONTHLY PAYMENTS PROPOSED BY THE PLAN
	IF DISPUTED. AMT. ADMITTED	BRIEF DESCRIPTION OF SECURITY IF ANY			

5

REMARKS:

194

SCHEDULE OF DEBTS
(Continued)

State the name of Creditor (including the last known holder of any negotiable instrument) and the residence or place of business of each creditor (if unknown, so state).

NAME, ADDRESS, ZIP CODE AND ACCOUNT NO. IF ANY	AMOUNT DUE OR CLAIMED BY CREDITOR	CLASSIFICATION OR CODES	MONTHLY PAYMENTS DUE PER CONTRACT	NUMBER OF INSTALLMENTS IN ARREARS	SPECIFIC PAYMENTS, IF ANY, TO BE MADE UNDER THE DEBTOR'S PLAN
					MONTHLY PAYMENTS PROPOSED BY THE PLAN
1	IF DISPUTED, AMT. ADMITTED	BRIEF DESCRIPTION OF SECURITY IF ANY			
REMARKS:					
NAME, ADDRESS, ZIP CODE AND ACCOUNT NO. IF ANY	AMOUNT DUE OR CLAIMED BY CREDITOR	CLASSIFICATION OR CODES	MONTHLY PAYMENTS DUE PER CONTRACT	NUMBER OF INSTALLMENTS IN ARREARS	MONTHLY PAYMENTS PROPOSED BY THE PLAN
2	IF DISPUTED, AMT. ADMITTED	BRIEF DESCRIPTION OF SECURITY IF ANY			
REMARKS:					
NAME, ADDRESS, ZIP CODE AND ACCOUNT NO. IF ANY	AMOUNT DUE OR CLAIMED BY CREDITOR	CLASSIFICATION OR CODES	MONTHLY PAYMENTS DUE PER CONTRACT	NUMBER OF INSTALLMENTS IN ARREARS	MONTHLY PAYMENTS PROPOSED BY THE PLAN
3	IF DISPUTED, AMT. ADMITTED	BRIEF DESCRIPTION OF SECURITY IF ANY			
REMARKS:					
NAME, ADDRESS, ZIP CODE AND ACCOUNT NO. IF ANY	AMOUNT DUE OR CLAIMED BY CREDITOR	CLASSIFICATION OR CODES	MONTHLY PAYMENTS DUE PER CONTRACT	NUMBER OF INSTALLMENTS IN ARREARS	MONTHLY PAYMENTS PROPOSED BY THE PLAN
4	IF DISPUTED, AMT. ADMITTED	BRIEF DESCRIPTION OF SECURITY IF ANY			
REMARKS:					

NAME, ADDRESS, ZIP CODE AND ACCOUNT NO. IF ANY	AMOUNT DUE OR CLAIMED BY CREDITOR	CLASSIFICATION OR CODES	MONTHLY PAYMENTS DUE PER CONTRACT	NUMBER OF INSTALLMENTS IN ARREARS	MONTHLY PAYMENTS PROPOSED BY THE PLAN
5	IF DISPUTED, AMT. ADMITTED	BRIEF DESCRIPTION OF SECURITY IF ANY			
REMARKS:					
6 NAME, ADDRESS, ZIP CODE AND ACCOUNT NO. IF ANY	AMOUNT DUE OR CLAIMED BY CREDITOR / IF DISPUTED, AMT. ADMITTED	CLASSIFICATION OR CODES / BRIEF DESCRIPTION OF SECURITY IF ANY	MONTHLY PAYMENTS DUE PER CONTRACT	NUMBER OF INSTALLMENTS IN ARREARS	MONTHLY PAYMENTS PROPOSED BY THE PLAN
REMARKS:					
7 NAME, ADDRESS, ZIP CODE AND ACCOUNT NO. IF ANY	AMOUNT DUE OR CLAIMED BY CREDITOR / IF DISPUTED, AMT. ADMITTED	CLASSIFICATION OR CODES / BRIEF DESCRIPTION OF SECURITY IF ANY	MONTHLY PAYMENTS DUE PER CONTRACT	NUMBER OF INSTALLMENTS IN ARREARS	MONTHLY PAYMENTS PROPOSED BY THE PLAN
REMARKS:					
8 NAME, ADDRESS, ZIP CODE AND ACCOUNT NO. IF ANY	AMOUNT DUE OR CLAIMED BY CREDITOR / IF DISPUTED, AMT. ADMITTED	CLASSIFICATION OR CODES / BRIEF DESCRIPTION OF SECURITY IF ANY	MONTHLY PAYMENTS DUE PER CONTRACT	NUMBER OF INSTALLMENTS IN ARREARS	MONTHLY PAYMENTS PROPOSED BY THE PLAN
REMARKS:					

TOTALS ON LAST PAGE ONLY

NO. OF CREDITORS	AMOUNT DUE OR CLAIMED	MONTHLY CONTRACT PAYMENTS	MONTHLY PAYMENTS PER PLAN

PAGE NO.

NAME OF DEBTOR _____

LIST ALL REAL ESTATE AND OTHER PROPERTY OWNED BY YOU OR YOUR SPOUSE AT DATE OF FILING OF ORIGINAL PETITION HEREIN.

EXCEPT AS NOTED

(A) ALL PERSONAL PROPERTY IS LOCATED AT THE RESIDENCE OF THE DEBTOR AS SHOWN ON THIS STATEMENT.

(B) ALL PROPERTY IS CO-OWNED BY THE DEBTOR AND SPOUSE, IF ANY, AND IS NOT CO-OWNED WITH ANY OTHER PERSON.

(C) THE DEBTOR IS UNABLE TO VERIFY WHICH ITEMS OF PERSONAL PROPERTY ARE EFFECTIVELY HYPOTHECATED TO CREDITORS.

DESCRIPTION OF REAL PROPERTY	PRESENT MARKET VALUE WITHOUT DEDUCTION FOR MORTGAGE OR SECURITY INTEREST	REMARKS, INDICATE ANY EXCEPTIONS TO THE STATEMENT ABOVE ATTACH ADDITIONAL MEMORANDUM IF NEEDED

THE TOTAL AMOUNT OF DEBT SECURED BY A LIEN ON THIS PROPERTY. $ _____

THE NET VALUE OF THE PROPERTY IN EXCESS OF LIENS. $ _____

IF THE INDEBTEDNESSES IS PAYABLE IN MONTHLY INSTALLMENTS HOW MUCH IS EACH INSTALLMENT ? $ _____

HOW MANY MONTHS ARE PAYMENTS IN DEFAULT. _____

THE NAME(S) OF THE LIENHOLDER(S). FULL NAME AND ADDRESS MUST BE ON LIST OF DEBTS.

PERSONAL AND OTHER PROPERTY	AMOUNT OF MORTGAGE OR OTHER SECURITY INTEREST ON THIS PROPERTY	NAME OF CREDITOR ABBREVIATE - FULL NAME & ADDRESS MUST BE ON LIST OF DEBTS
AUTOMOBILES OR OTHER VEHICLES GIVE YEAR AND MAKE		

HOUSEHOLD GOODS

PERSONAL EFFECTS

OTHER (SPECIFY)

TAX REFUNDS   INDICATE WHAT TAX REFUNDS (INCOME OR OTHER), IF ANY, TO WHICH EITHER YOU OR YOUR SPOUSE ARE ENTITLED. (GIVE PARTICULARS INCLUDING INFORMATION AS TO ANY REFUNDS PAYABLE JOINTLY WITH ANY OTHER PERSON.)

BANK ACCOUNTS AND SAFE DEPOSIT BOXES   IF YOU OR YOUR SPOUSE CURRENTLY HAVE ANY BANK OR SAVINGS AND LOAN ACCOUNTS, CHECKING, OR SAVINGS, GIVE NAME AND ADDRESS OF BANK, NATURE OF ACCOUNT, CURRENT BALANCE. NAME AND ADDRESS OF EACH PERSON AUTHORIZED TO MAKE WITHDRAWALS FROM THE ACCOUNT. (IF NONE, SO STATE.)

TOTAL →

EXEMPTION ELECTION

The Debtor _____
                    (name)

elects to have exemptions determined pursuant to (Check one)

☐ 11 U.S.C. 522(b) (1) (Federal Exemption)

☐ 11 U.S.C. 522(b) (2) (State Exemption), and

Any lien which may be avoided pursuant to 11 USC 522(f) shall be avoided for the benefit of the debtor(s).

PROPERTY CLAIMED AS EXEMPT

Type of property	Location, description, and so far as relevant to the claim of exemption, present use of property	Reference to statute creating the exemption	Value claimed exempt
			$
	Total		Total

PROPERTY NOT OTHERWISE SCHEDULED

Type of property	Description and location	Market value of debtor's interest
a. Property transferred under assignment for benefit of creditors, within 90 days prior to filing of petition (specify date of assignment, name and address of assignee, amount realized therefrom by the assignee, and disposition of proceeds so far as known to debtor)		$
b. Legal or equitable interest in Property of any kind not otherwise scheduled		
Total		

FORECLOSURES, EXECUTIONS AND ATTACHMENTS

IS ANY OF YOUR OR YOUR SPOUSE'S PROPERTY, INCLUDING REAL ESTATE, INVOLVED IN FORECLOSURE PROCEEDINGS IN OR OUT OF COURT? IF SO IDENTIFY THE PROPERTY AND THE PERSON FORECLOSING.

HAS ANY OF YOUR OR YOUR SPOUSE'S PROPERTY OR INCOME BEEN ATTACHED, GARNISHED OR SEIZED UNDER ANY LEGAL OR EQUITABLE PROCESS WITHIN THE 90 DAYS IMMEDIATELY PRECEDING THE FILING OF THE ORIGINAL PETITION HEREIN? (IF SO, DESCRIBE THE PROPERTY SEIZED, OR PERSON GARNISHED AND AT WHOSE SUIT).

TRANSFERS, REPOSSESSIONS AND RETURNS

HAS ANY OF YOUR OR YOUR SPOUSE'S PROPERTY BEEN TRANSFERRED, RETURNED, REPOSSESSED OR SEIZED BY THE SELLER OR BY ANY OTHER PARTY, INCLUDING A LANDLORD, DURING THE ( ) DAYS IMMEDIATELY PRECEDING THE FILING OF THE ORIGINAL PETITION HEREIN? (IF SO, GIVE PARTICULARS INCLUDING THE NAME AND ADDRESS OF THE PARTY GETTING THE PROPERTY AND ITS DESCRIPTION AND VALUE.)

PRIOR BANKRUPTCY OR DEBTOR RELIEF PROCEEDING

WHAT PROCEEDINGS UNDER TITLE 11, U.S.C. OR ITS ANTECEDENT STATUTES HAVE PREVIOUSLY BEEN BROUGHT BY OR AGAINST YOU OR YOUR SPOUSE? (STATE THE LOCATION OF THE COURT, THE NATURE AND NUMBER OF EACH PROCEEDING, THE DATE IT WAS FILED, AND WHETHER A DISCHARGE WAS GRANTED OR REFUSED, THE PROCEEDING WAS DISMISSED, OR A COMPOSITION, ARRANGEMENT, OR PLAN WAS CONFIRMED).

Index